JUNE THE PRUNE AND LADY BIRD

Cancer Stinks! Kids and Pets Cracking the Power Code

GRACIE BRADFORD

Web: http://www.AuthorGracieBradford.com/
PO Box 841148
Pearland, Texas 77584
Cover design by SelfPubBookCovers.com/NICECOVERS-kt
Interior photos © 2015 copyright from shutterstock.com

Copyright © August 2016 Gracie Bradford

All rights reserved. No part of this book may be used or reproduced in any manner without written permission, except in the case of brief quotations embedded in critical articles or reviews.

ISBN-13: 9781534707016
ISBN-10: 1534707018
Library of Congress Control Number: 2016910479
CreateSpace Independent Publishing Platform
North Charleston, South Carolina

JUNE THE PRUNE AND LADY BIRD

Go to:
http://amzn.to/2hav66c
For some Reviews

Goto:
http://lamzi.to/shwbbe
for some reviews

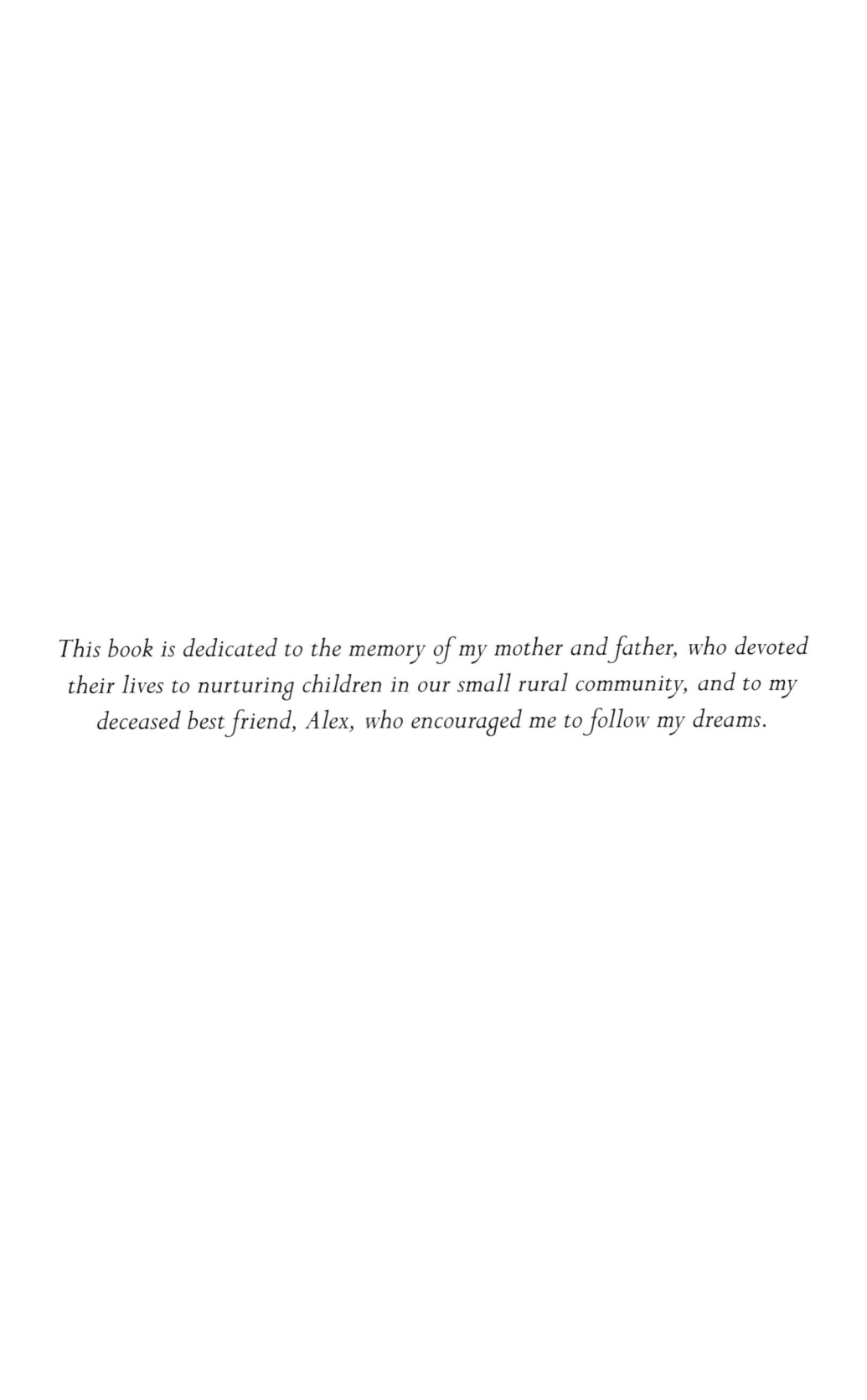

This book is dedicated to the memory of my mother and father, who devoted their lives to nurturing children in our small rural community, and to my deceased best friend, Alex, who encouraged me to follow my dreams.

NOTE TO READERS:

The book deals with serious subjects such as life-threatening illness, parental neglect, mental illness, blended families, and power of believing, which profoundly affect parents as well as teachers who manage children behaviors in the classroom. Often unrecognized is the value of pet therapy in the healing process and grandparents in the child rearing process. Many children turn to pets as their only companion. Forty-eight percent of U.S. average households have at least one pet (Source: U.S. Census Bureau and U.S. Department of Housing and Urban Development, 2013 American Housing Survey, Revised May 12, 2015). According to the U.S. 2009 Census Bureau, over seven million children lived with at least one grandparent, a sixty-four percent increase since 1991 (seventeen percent Black, fourteen percent Hispanic, nine percent White). According to the U.S. Census Bureau Report release number CB14-324, fifty-six percent of children experienced a transition related to change in family structure between 2008 and 2011, a number which continues to grow. Equally as striking is that seventeen thousand forty-three mothers are in growing cohabiting relationships with joint biological children under twelve years old.

Although June is ten years old, the author recommends parents reading the book first then determine if the content is too intense for their middle school child.

*We do not need magic to transform our world.
We carry all the power we need inside ourselves
already. We have the power to imagine better.*

—J. K. Rowling, author of the Harry Potter series

CONTENTS

	Acknowledgments	xiii
	Prologue	xv
Chapter 1	When "No" Really Means "Yes"	1
	The Power of Persuasion	19
Chapter 2	Happiness in the Sky	20
	The Power of Silence	25
Chapter 3	Youth Trumps Wisdom	26
	The Power of Laughter	34
Chapter 4	The Shadow of Reverse Lens	35
	The Power of Companionship	43
Chapter 5	Back Home to Small Town, USA	44
	The Power of Grandma's Love	47
Chapter 6	Truth Collides with Reality	48
	The Power of Body Language	52
Chapter 7	June Finds Inspiration	53
	The Power of Positive Thinking	57

Chapter 8	Food from Mars	58
Chapter 9	Chemo and Rad Partnership	63
	The Power of Inspiration	68
Chapter 10	A Visit from Captain Jeff	69
	The Power of Willpower	83

	Epilogue	85
	Contact the Author	87
	About the Author	93

ACKNOWLEDGMENTS

I wish to acknowledge Isaiah Specks, president of MBradford Management Associates LLC Youth Advisory Board, for encouraging me to complete this book and for his devotion and tenacity in pushing me beyond my limits.

I would also like to acknowledge my editor, Lora, who had long-lasting patience in the rewrite. I am grateful to my media friends in two groups, who responded to my question about how pets impacted their return on investment—the stories were amazing. I would like to thank the following subject-matter experts who peer-reviewed specific chapters: Marion Hubbard, clinical dietitian, Detroit, Michigan, and Lizzie Ferguson, lead teacher, Alma J. Brown Lab School of Grambling State University, Grambling, Louisiana.

PROLOGUE

Every year, June and her brother, Alex, take a road trip with their grandmother. She insists that the children call her "G-Mom" because she does not think she is a real granny at her age. Some trips are long, and others trips are short. This year, G-Mom has decided to fly June and Alex out of the country. G-Mom thinks it is time for her two favorite grandchildren to see the world.

June is a feisty ten-year-old tomboy who enjoys gymnastics, softball, football, and dancing. She spends every waking hour she can carve out participating in outdoor competitive contact team sports. June once had long black hair with curls. When she was six years old, she convinced her mom to cut her hair into a short style that made it easier for her to do her routines in gymnastics. June was born when Alex was two years old. June never met her dad. Her mother became very hostile anytime June asked why she did not have a dad like her friend Kayla.

Amy would say, "He's probably somewhere with his other children. You need to stop asking me about your father. I told you many times that he will never be in our lives."

June secretly cried every time they talked about her father. She could not understand why he left her mom, Alex and her alone. June did not grasp that her father did not leave since he was never there. June knew that her mom hated her and did not ever show her any love; never hugged her; never complimented her; never smiled with her.

June would say, "Why did she have me if she did not want me?"

To June, the only love in her life was her brother, Alex, and her dog, Lady Bird. June and Alex spent many nights home alone while their mom went out partying. One day June asked her mom if she loved her. The rage that came from Amy confirmed for June that Amy did not want her and was sorry that she was born. In spite of her mother's behavior towards her, June learned to show love and affection to her mother.

Alex, on the other hand, is the complete opposite. Alex does not like to do anything involving burning energy. He prefers indoor, noncompetitive individual sports. He spends his free time playing video games, reading comic books, and daydreaming about the pretty little girl next door and about his next big invention. Unlike June, Alex is a twelve-year-old with red hair and green eyes that change from brown to blue when in the sunlight. Alex's father came around sometime on holidays for the first two years then he just stopped showing up. Alex had not established a father-son bond with him and did not miss his dad when he stopped coming around. Alex had not seen his father for ten years.

G-Mom is an eighty-year-old who sports a short haircut and walks five miles every day. Like June, she loves to dance. She does not act or look like she is eighty years old, except for the salt-and-pepper hair. For the past fifteen years, she lived alone except when

JUNE THE PRUNE AND LADY BIRD

Alex stayed with her. She progressed to the top of her professional career at an early age and continued until retirement.

Lady Bird is an aging beagle and June's trusted companion. She suffers severely from anxiety and depression when June leaves her alone for more than a week. Lady Bird is like an overprotective big sister, instantly sensing when something is not right with June.

June and Alex often played in the backyard. One day, Alex heard a sound coming from the bushes. He thought it might be a bird that had fallen from the tree. When Alex went over to investigate, Alex saw a scrawny puppy with big blue eyes, long ears with a cute combination of the brown, beige, and white coat. The animal looked like he had not eaten for weeks. The puppy is so tiny than other beagles his size. June and Alex secretly cared for the little puppy hiding him under the porch in an old wagon. Alex would fill his pockets with food after each meal. June would save leftover food when she cleaned the kitchen in order not to reveal the presence of the puppy. Alex referred to the puppy as "the bird." The puppy started to grow and would prance like a model June had seen on TV modeling a brown and white fur coat. June started referring to the puppy as "the lady" to keep from revealing the puppy. One day, their mom, Amy, was sitting on the patio watching June and Alex on the swing. She kept hearing movement under the porch. Amy got up to investigate when she discovered the puppy.

Amy, "Alright, where did this puppy come from and how long has she lived under here?"

June blurted out, "Lady was lost and had no place to live."

Alex chimed in and said, "We thought Bird was a lost bird but realized it was a puppy."

xvii

Amy looked at both of the kids knowing she was not getting the full story. Amy said, "How long has this puppy been here?"

In unison, Alex said, "Bird has been here for two months, and June said, "Lady has been here for two months."

Amy asked, "Since you call her "Bird" and you call her "Lady", is there another puppy under this porch?"

June quickly replied, "No, it's just Lady." Thus, the hidden puppy instantly became Lady Bird. Amy pondered if she should allow the puppy to stay. The kids seem to enjoy the dog. After all, they cared for her for two secret months. Amy told Alex and June the puppy could stay but the moment she caught the puppy in her room, the kitchen, or living room, she would have to go. At the time, Amy did not realize the powerful impact this lost lonely little puppy would have on the life of her children.

June and Alex never dream or imagine that this might be their first and maybe last out-of-the-country trip and last road trip with their grandmother, G-Mom, for a very long time to come.

The "Thing" creeps in under the dark of night, even outsmarting Lady Bird. It comes without warning, and does not announce its arrival. The tunnel of darkness seems to have no escape. Who will host the "Thing"—June, her parents, her brother, or her grandmother? Can the family survive the raging attack? Will they grow closer and help each other? June's story is compelling at times, riveting at times, unbelievable at times, and scary at times, but she shares her story from the depths of her soul. The bravery is captivating!

As an established leader in healthcare, I was always examining how well and how often my managers used upward power on me. I also vividly remember practicing use of upward power on my older sisters and brothers and my senior executive. While writing the story of June, I saw a familiar theme of power emerging in each chapter demonstrating the potential to influence the behavior of my main characters especially June, Alex, G-Mom, Amy and Lady Bird hence the development of the power codes dogs and children unknowingly use that could resonate with grown-ups. My mind kept going back to how pets and humans heal each other.

The five types of authority frequently used in business are coercive power, expert power, informational power, reward power, connection power, and referent power. I focused on referent power which is the ability to convey a sense of personal acceptance or approval over another or cause an action or influence the behavior of others. My light bulb went off when I saw a direct correlation between leadership power and dog-kid power.

Cheers!

I AM ….

Chapter 1

WHEN "NO" REALLY MEANS "YES"

June, her brother, and the rest of the family were sitting around the table, eating their favorite ice cream for an evening snack. Their mother, Amy, had a tradition of serving ice cream every day for five days leading up to a holiday. Rewarding them with ice cream was one good thing that Amy did do for the children.

June lived in a small country town in Louisiana, located in the Deep South. The population was less than three thousand, and everyone knew each other. The town had one stop light, one grocery market, one school for all grades, and one small playground, but no banks and no shopping malls.

That day had been particularly exciting for June because G-Mom, who lived in the big state of Texas, had come home for the holiday. Thanksgiving was always a very special holiday for the family. It was the time of year when the leaves turned shades of deep orange with sprinkles of brown and turkeys tried to escape the traditional turkey hunt from all the hunters in the community.

By the age of ten, June had learned to cook by default and to take care of the household chores. She cared for her older brother throughout most of his school years. Even though Alex was two years older than June, he was so much smaller in stature and did not seem to fit in very well with children his age. June took on the role of big sister and in some ways, his mother figure. She knew when G-Mom arrived, she would have someone to help with completing the Thanksgiving dinner and her grandmother could give her a break from being the grown-up. She often daydreamed about what it would be like to be a child in a family like her friend Kayla's. Kayla's mother treated June as if June was her daughter. She drove both girls to school every morning chatting about world events. Kayla's father often helped with repairs for the house and took the girls out for ice cream.

June always loved when G-Mom was around because her mother's behavior would go from mean to calm in a split second. June thought her mother was two different people. She wondered if her mother was afraid of G-Mom.

June and G-Mom would find a way to escape from the rest of the family to spend hours just talking about nothing and sharing secrets with each other. Amy did not like it when G-Mom came home because she thought June would tell her everything that was going on in the household. It was not necessary for June to reveal the family secrets because G-Mom had a sixth sense, like the family's beagle, Lady Bird.

While the family conversation in the sitting room was robust, June was not listening but daydreaming about what her granny would give her. She always received special presents when G-Mom came to visit. She was hoping for a new football or maybe several new pairs of jeans like her friend Kayla had. Amy left the family and went back into her bedroom. Alex had retreated to his room. When G-Mom called Alex back and asked him to join them, June became a little jealous, even though she wasn't listening carefully to the conversation. June did not want her brother infringing upon her time with G-Mom. She decided to keep quiet to see what was about to happen.

G-Mom put her arms around both children and said, "We are going to tour Europe for about fifteen days to see some unique sites."

June looked at G-Mom, wondering whom she was referring to as "we." Every year, June and Alex took a road trip with G-Mom but never to another country. June just smiled and said, "That's nice. Which group are you traveling with this time?"

June knew G-Mom considered herself to be a world traveler. She had three favorite travel tour groups. One consisted of a group of young adults between the ages of thirty and forty years old. G-Mom joined this group as the "seasoned citizen" tour guide. She always had so much fun with this group, mostly trying to understand what they were talking about in their conversations. She also enjoyed showing them the sites and demonstrating that she still had the ability to communicate well even at her age.

The next group consisted of people from all over the United States, and the people had diverse backgrounds and ethnicities. She particularly enjoyed the diverse tour group. It was led by an anthropologist, who knew everything about the places they traveled. G-Mom had traveled to all continents except Antarctica. She had gone on over a dozen trips with this group and loved every minute of her time away from home, especially with the gentlemen in the group. Most of the travelers in this group were about the same age as she was or younger.

The third group that G-Mom traveled with was a little unusual for an eighty-year-old grandmother. She was the most popular chaperone for the high school trips in the city where she lived. If she did not volunteer to go, the kids volunteered her. The teens liked having her because she would allow them to explore in groups but gave very strict guidelines for them to follow. Rarely did any of the teens disobey after one student experienced the wrath of G-Mom while on a tour. The teachers loved having her around because it gave them the opportunity to vacation rather than constantly watch the children. G-Mom always made a goodie box for each child to stuff into his or her backpack. No two boxes were the same. Inside each box was an inspirational or motivational quote from a famous person in time. The children enjoyed discussing their quotes and trying to determine what message G-Mom was sending them.

When G-Mom said she would be taking June and Alex with her on the diverse group, June screamed thunderously with excitement. Alex continued watching the movie on his iPad. Amy ran to the sitting room to see what was wrong.

June shouted, "G-Mom plans to take Alex and me to Europe for fifteen days!" June turned to her mom with so much excitement on her face because she had never been on an airplane.

Alex just said, "OK, whatever," and he shrugged his shoulders.

June's mom, Amy, was looking at her mother with piercing eyes, wondering when G-Mom had discussed the trip with her. Amy said calmly, "Mom, these are *my* children, and you can't make that kind of decision without talking to me first." She was speaking calmly, but June knew she was furious.

June could not understand why her mom was so angry. After all, G-Mom would be paying for the trip, school would be out, they had no plans for the summer, and her mother would be at work every day. June had seen her mom angry on many occasions and could detect the signs very quickly. She rarely, however, had seen her mom react that way with G-Mom.

G-Mom was a trustworthy grandmother. The children stayed with her all the time during summer breaks and when Amy had to go out of town. Alex had lived with G-Mom on and off most of his young life. When June's mom said the children could not go, June and Alex stormed out of the room and ran to sit on the swing in the backyard. Alex follows June's lead when he senses conflict. Lady Bird dutifully followed the kids to the backyard, not understanding who made June so angry. When things would go wrong in the household, June and Alex would retreat to the backyard and hide behind the swing or just sit and turn, letting the wind hit their faces. Both immediately pushed the swings as fast as they could.

June knew Alex was angry because he was pushing the swing unusually fast. Then he suddenly jumped off the swing and climbed to the top of the tree. June was worried that he would hurt himself. She finally talked him into coming down so they could come up with strategies to convince their mom that going with G-Mom was a good idea. Both of the children knew it was a daunting task convincing their mom to allow them to go with their grandmother for fifteen days to Europe. After all, who would do the cooking, cleaning, and shopping for Amy if June was not around to do it? June knew the real reason that her mom had said no, but her brother was unaware of the jealousy their mom had toward them. Every time their grandmother did something for June and Alex and did not include their mom, she would put up roadblocks. Their grandmother also knew her daughter very well and was not surprised at her reaction, but June's brother was very confused and just did not understand his mom's behavior.

While sitting in the backyard, June decided that her brother had gotten wise enough to hear about the years their mom had

had to go through struggles, which June thought had made her the way she was toward them and explained why she was always so angry.

Amy was tall and stunning, except for her mean personality. She had an unusual illness that caused her to be out-of-work for many months. June's mother referred to her illness as "the Thing" but would never explain any further to June. Amy had a type of depression that changed her behavior in an instant. She took medications that made her sleep for long periods of time. Amy's addiction to painkillers showed up every time she became upset with June. June instantly knew to put distance between her mom's right swing and her head. June learned how to stay out of harm's way and how to protect Alex and Lady Bird. To June, her mom was a ticking time bomb. In spite of her behavior, June loved her mom very much. Then, a year after getting better from her illness, she had allowed her anger to get out of control, gotten into a fight with a coworker, and been jailed for a year. Alex had been staying with G-Mom in another state and did not realize that his mother was not living at home. It was not unusual for his mom not to contact him for months at a time.

June had stayed with an aunt during the year of her mother's incarceration, so she could continue participating in her sports activities. G-Mom sheltered the children every time Amy got into trouble. G-Mom did not want anyone to know she had raised a daughter who turned out to be such an embarrassment. Instead, G-Mom would sweep all of the embarrassing things her daughter did under the rug. She told everyone that she had gone on an extended vacation when Amy was in jail. When Amy was sick, G-Mom would hire a home-health nurse to care for her rather than have Amy come to live with her. G-Mom felt she was protecting the children.

June also decided to tell her brother about the relationship between their mom and their mom's mother. Amy was a single parent and had had to raise June and Alex alone, although her mom provided money whenever asked. The children did not know their father but had experienced many "uncles" who came and went. June had seen her mother cry often. Her mother was never satisfied with her jobs and was angry all the time. Sometimes, she would scream at June for no good reason. The only time June saw her mother happy was when the song "Purple Rain" came on the radio. Amy would sing along with the music at the top of her voice, swaying left to right. Her face would light up like a Christmas tree. She smiled and even threw June a warm look.

June always protected her mother, shielding the neighbors from any bad things that occurred in the home, even though June was just ten years old herself. There were so many times when June felt she was the mother instead of the child.

When June was eight years old and her mother was recovering from the "Thing", June had to take over most of the household chores. June would get up at dawn to go collect the eggs from the chicken coop. She would cook breakfast, put it on a tray, and take it to her mom's bedroom. She knew she had done a good job if the juice did not get splashed in her face, the toast did not get thrown at her, or she did not hear a succession of four-letter words too horrible to repeat. After June finished serving her mother's breakfast, she ate, washed the dishes, and cleaned the house.

Before leaving for school, June would make sure Lady Bird had food and water near the big oak tree in the center of the backyard. June did not dare to leave Lady Bird indoors.

While Amy was sick, June walked to her neighbor's house to catch a ride to school. Even though Amy never said anything nice to or about her daughter, June seemed happy and acted like a "normal" child when around the neighbors. When no one was around, she would spend most of her free time in her room reading books. Sometimes June would lie in the bed just looking up at the ceiling and hoping that something good would rain down over her life. June wondered where her father might be and why he never came to visit her and her brother. Before leaving the house to participate in after-school activities, June prepared dinner for Amy, helped her to get dressed, and set up a snack tray on the table.

Because June was such an obedient student, the teachers made sure she always had a ride to school for the extracurricular activities. June never discussed what was going on inside her cozy little yellow house at the end of Autumn Street. Even after Amy's recovery, June continued to do all the household chores. Everyone at the corner store knew June and helped her to count out the money for the weekly groceries. The old man sitting outside the shop walked with June and Lady Bird to help carry the groceries home. June would thank him and set the bags on the porch. She never allowed anyone inside the house for fear of Amy's reaction.

Last year, June's mom got married for the first time at the age of thirty-five to a man ten years her senior and moved him and his children into her home. Amy is a college graduate who majored in Marketing and Advertising. She has not worked in her profession since graduation. Most of her jobs have been minimum wage positions. Alex was born immediately after Amy graduated from college and June was born two years later. Amy was a single mom working two jobs to help take care of the two kids and paying back student loans. The children father did not pay child support. Amy stood six feet tall with long black-brown hair, slim, and was an eye-catching caramel colored beauty in looks. She dressed like a fashion model.

Amy's new husband majored in Criminal Justice and worked as a police officer. He was shorter than Amy and extremely overweight. He was a chain smoker and used profanity far too often around the family. All of his children had different mothers. He had a no-nonsense demeanor with an ego as large as the state of Texas. He made it known that his kids were smarter than Alex and June. Rather than defending her children, Amy accepted his position on the intellect of the children even though June was a straight "A" student.

Amy wanted to make her new husband a dad to June and Alex. But June knew that the new husband did not like them, did not want them around, and hated Lady Bird. The blended family went from two children to eight overnight. All of his children were teenagers, except for the oldest son. June and Alex did not readily establish a bond with the new brothers and sisters nor did the new brothers and sisters show any interest in building a relationship with them. June and Alex did not appreciate having to share their things with the stepchildren. June explained to her brother that things would be different from when it was just Mom and them. She told Alex that everything would be divided now among eight children instead of two. Their mom made it very clear that they had to share everything, including their clothes, toys, phones, bathrooms, closet spaces, designer tennis shoes, and yes, her softball mitt. June could not imagine how she would manage to take care of eight children in one house.

While Amy was dating her new husband, June and Alex noticed how she would cuddle with his children but not with them. Their mother laughed and played around with his children but not with Alex and June. Amy would attend her boyfriend's children's sports events but never took the time to attend June's gymnastic events or her softball games. June overheard her teachers talking about how her mother paid more attention to her stepchildren than to June. It made her sad to know other people noticed her mother's indifference.

June became acutely aware their new life living with two parents instead of one parent had gotten worse rather than better. June longed for the day her mother would show her love and compassion and treat her like the child she was. She just wanted a normal childhood, like the other kids in the community. June could never understand why her mother did not love her.

Both of the children pondered sheltering Lady Bird, who did not like strangers in the house. Lady Bird had been with June since she was a baby. Alex and June worried about what would happen to Lady Bird if they were going to Europe for so long.

Lady Bird had become June's best friend and protector. June always felt safe when Lady Bird guarded her door. She would take Lady Bird on long walks every morning, oblivious to the danger lurking around every corner in her now drug-infested neighborhood. All of the people were friendly to June. They knew that Lady Bird would forge a vicious attack if anyone tried to mess with June, based on one incident when a man attempted to lure June into his van. The word spread quickly about how Lady Bird fended off the attacker. If it rained, June would dress Lady in her raincoat and umbrella hat to keep her from getting wet. When it was sweltering, June would put furry little boots on Lady Bird's feet to keep the hot pavement from burning her feet. June fed Lady Bird a special vegetarian diet and gave her ginger-snap cookies when she did something unusually caring. Anywhere you saw June, you would see Lady Bird.

When Amy was sick, Lady Bird rode to school in the front seat of the neighbor's van every morning and anxiously waited with her head out the car window when it was time to pick June up from school. Lady Bird was not allowed in their stepfather's vehicle at any time. Amy had started insisting that June leave Lady Bird in the backyard rather than on the enclosed patio.

As soon as they arrived home from school, June went to finish her homework in her room while Lady Bird guarded her door, even though Amy did not want her inside the house.

June knew Lady Bird was losing her eyesight. She and Alex had come up with a plan to maybe leave Lady Bird in a safe and loving environment away from their new family. They knew that their mom would not take care of her the way they did. At the same time, they did not dare ask one of the stepbrothers or stepsisters to take care of Lady Bird while they were away. June considered asking G-Mom to take Lady Bird with them, like they did when they went on their short trips within the United States. But Alex convinced her it was not a good idea since they did not know what to expect on the Europe trip.

G-Mom knew that her biological grandchildren needed her love and support and that she had to give it to them at a distance. She knew that after the marriage, her daughter did not want her in their lives. June explained to her brother that G-Mom could not openly do for them anymore, for her mom wanted G-Mom to do the same for the other children in the household. Even though her brother was older than she was, June was wiser in years.

Alex did not understand and said, "But they are not her grandchildren."

The conversation was getting too complicated for June to explain, so she suggested that they just play outside for a while and let G-Mom find a way to turn "no" into "yes," using her magic of persuasion. June had confidence in G-Mom.

June believed that her grandmother could do anything she wanted. She knew how good her grandmother was. She also knew that her grandmother loved her daughter very much and would try to respect her wishes but would also do the right thing when it came to her and her brother. For a moment, June considered going to listen at the door to her mom and grandmother talking—or rather, her mom shouting. But she knew her grandmother did not approve of eavesdropping.

June reminded her brother why she believed her grandmother would make their mom change her mind. What she could not explain was why her mom was insisting that G-Mom take all of the children. June knew her grandmother well enough to know that would never happen on this trip or any other because G-Mom saw the difference in how her daughter treated her own children and the stepchildren.

G-Mom had used stories to get her points across so many times with June and Alex. She rarely raised her voice and always had a quiet and calming demeanor when talking to anyone. You had to listen to her full stories to find the lessons she often taught to her daughter and her grandchildren. They were amazing! G-Mom never met a child who did not cling to her for affection, love, support, and gifts—except one, whom she was currently working on.

G-Mom grew up in a community with many small children she had to babysit. She also worked with the kids throughout her career and as a volunteer in the community. G-Mom was a born educator and had outstanding parenting skills. She treated every child as if he or she were her own. That was why when children saw her, they would run up and hug her. It was as if G-Mom had a bright light surrounding her and signaling to the children she was their friend. Even the new children added to her daughter's family became attached to her, which made Amy jealous.

G-Mom was well aware of her daughter's insane jealousy toward anyone G-Mom showed affection and attention. She knew that her daughter, who was almost like an only child, was spoiled. There were ten years between Amy's age and the age of her only brother. Even as an adult, her daughter got whatever she wanted up until the time she made the decision to become a blended family. Then, G-Mom showered her two grandchildren with extras that she felt they were lacking. Amy did not think her children lacked anything. She wanted her mother to believe that she and her new husband could take care of the eight children equally. What Amy forgot was that G-Mom had a sixth sense. G-Mom knew things and could sense when something was not right.

When Amy was growing up, she told her playmates that her mother had eyes in the back of her head and on the side of her face and could see through her nose like a telescope. They all believed her because G-Mom was able to tell them no even before they could ask or tell them to stop doing things with her back turned to them. The children could not see those extra sets of eyes, but they always knew they were there.

G-Mom had planned this trip for years before her daughter's marriage. It was called a grandma-grandchildren trip to anyplace they wanted to go. It was supposed to be the grand tour of travel. June wondered what story G-Mom would tell her mom to get her to change her mind. June was confident that her grandmother would soon come out the back door and let them know the trip was on.

G-Mom struggled to find the right story to tell her daughter. She was so disappointed in her daughter's behavior but did not tell her. It broke G-Mom's heart to see her only daughter disrespecting her. G-Mom realized that she should have discussed the decision with her daughter before mentioning it to her grandchildren, but that was no excuse for this behavior.

G-Mom was somewhat confused over her daughter's reaction because her daughter had been involved in the discussion and planning of an out-of-country trip for the children over two years earlier. Amy had showed much excitement when hearing about G-Mom's trips every time G-Mom returned. G-Mom considered admitting her mistake and thought maybe she should apologize to her daughter. But she knew her daughter so well. She knew that an apology would not work and that it would only make Amy dig her heels in deeper.

So, G-Mom decided to tell the story of when she sent Amy to Africa to study for a semester abroad while she was in college. Amy even insisted that her brother quit his job to come with her as her protector. G-Mom added to the story with the reminder she had sent Amy's brother to India with his high school class. Her mother emphasized the educational experience and the fun they had had, as well as the sacrifice she had made for her and her brother to learn about other cultures and how other people lived in countries not like where they lived. In her story, she talked about her life and how she had made a promise to herself that her children would receive more exposure to the world than she had had the opportunity to experience herself at a young age.

G-Mom talked about the road trips that she and her daughter's children had taken and why they had chosen those places. She emphasized the success that her daughter's children had in school and how these trips contributed to them making good grades and being respected by their peers. She added to the story how important it was for the children to move out of their current environment for a while to give the newlyweds space to get to know each other and, in this case, to give Amy time to get to know the new children added to the family. G-Mom was smart and knew how to make her daughter feel guilty and change her mind without scolding her.

Amy was getting angrier with her mother with every sentence because she knew what she was doing. Her mother never failed. Amy knew the best thing for her was to stay quiet and listen.

G-Mom thought about just telling her daughter that her grandchildren would take the trip—end of discussion! But she had decided to rise above and appeal to her daughter's inner soul. She knew somewhere deep down, the daughter that she had raised was still present; she just needed to find a way to penetrate beyond the major invasion of jealousy that had overtaken her. G-Mom also knew that her daughter usually did not change her mind readily without making others believe that it was her idea to change her decision. G-Mom knew who had the influence in the family, and her daughter knew it also but would never admit that her mom was the voice of reason.

After finishing the story with her daughter, G-Mom walked around the room, pointing at pictures on the wall and emphasizing the smiles on her grandchildren's faces when they went to the Grand Canyon and to Niagara Falls. She moved further around the room and pointed at the photo of her daughter, who went on a cruise that G-Mom financed with ten other family members and her best friend for her twenty-first birthday. She smiled as she pointed out all the famous celebrities Amy had had the opportunity to meet and take pictures with.

When G-Mom got to Amy's wedding pictures, she deliberately paused and remembered the conversation she had had with Amy before her marriage. G-Mom knew that the marriage would not bring happiness for Amy. She also knew that Amy would never be the same. Her fear was that Amy would get worse. Nevertheless, she had to continue to convince Amy to let the children travel with her.

G-Mom would start all her sentences with "Do you remember when" and slowly moved from one picture to another until she stopped at the last picture of her mother, lying on the hospital bed. Tears formed in G-Mom's eyes at the thought of the time she flew her mother to Chicago for Taste of Chicago. Her mother had never before left the small community in which she lived. G-Mom stood there for a while and then turned to her daughter and said, "Do you remember when..."

It was at that moment that G-Mom penetrated and broke the barrier of selfishness, jealousy, and pride with her daughter just long enough to get her to allow the children to go on the trip. Although it was G-Mom's intent for her story to get Amy to change her mind and say yes to the trip, she achieved so much more that bright sunny day in her daughter's home. Amy wanted to walk over and hug G-Mom, but instead, she walked out into the backyard and called the children.

Amy gave both kids a big hug, squeezing them tightly, and told them how lucky they were to have a grandmother who was able and willing to take them out of the country for fifteen days. Amy admitted she was hurt that she had not been asked to go with them but knew she needed to stay home to take care of their stepsisters and stepbrothers. She then told the children that she thought about everything and decided maybe it was a good idea for them to take the trip that year out of the country with their grandmother without their stepbrothers and stepsisters.

Amy told her children about all the places she and her brother had traveled when they were growing up and talked about all the places her mother had visited. She told them that their grandmother was a world traveler, and her intent was to go to all continents in her lifetime. Amy explained that this would be the first of many trips out of the country. She said she hoped they would learn from this journey how important it was to speak foreign languages and understand why she had insisted that they take a foreign language throughout middle school. Amy told the children that they would learn a lot about traveling and to pay attention to their grandmother because "she has three sets of eyes in her head. She sees everything you do and knows when you are doing something you have no business doing. I trust her to take you all on this trip because you are her little monsters."

They hugged their mom tightly and started talking about what they would wear, getting passports, which friends they would call, and what research they needed to do before taking the trip. June and Alex ran to tell G-Mom thanks, but the kitchen was empty. They turned to their mom and asked where their grandmother was.

She said casually, "She left with her friends. We can discuss everything with her when she returns this afternoon."

June turned to her brother, gave him a high five, winked, and said, "That's our G-Mom, still the best!" June liked this side of her mother, although she and Alex rarely experienced such pleasantness.

When the children left the backyard, Amy started thinking about her own mother's upbringing. Her mother was the middle of nine children, four older than she was and four younger. She did not have a childhood because she had to care for the four younger children from age twelve. Amy's grandparents had an elementary school education but were wiser than most people she knew. Amy's mother finished high school and told her parents she wanted to go to college. Although they supported her desires, they did not have money to send another child to college because one was already in college.

Amy's mother was determined and announced to her parents that she would pay all of her college expenses. Amy recalled her mother telling how she picked black-eyed peas, blueberries, and peaches every summer, saving all her money to pay her way through college herself. Amy's mom finished college and went on to get two graduate degrees, which she financed with her blood, sweat, and tears. After reflecting for several hours, Amy ended up crying uncontrollably. She had not thought about the struggles of her mother or the sacrifices she had made for her and her brother in a long time. For a fleeting moment, Amy understood the drive and love her mother had for her children. She could clearly see at that moment why her mother had exposed them to the better side of life.

Crack 1

THE POWER OF PERSUASION

Kids pull things out of you that you already know and package it in a way that they can use it to become powerful in your life.

19

Chapter 2

HAPPINESS IN THE SKY

The day finally came for June, Alex, and G-Mom to board the airplane leaving Lady Bird with G-Mom's son. The tour group went to Budapest, Hungary; Mannheim, German; Vienna, Austria; Salzburg, Austria; Lucern, Switzerland, Munich, Germany; and Innsbruck, Austria to see as much of Europe as possible in the weeks they had to visit. Europe in the summer offered many sites of interest for the adults and kids. G-Mom wanted her grandchildren to see what she had seen when she took the trip several years earlier to the Christmas market, but they did not have time to get ready to leave within a month and could not make the Christmas market trip with G-Mom.

June and her brother both had their iPads and iPhones so they could take as many pictures as possible. Of course, G-Mom only had a disposable camera for taking pictures. She smiled when Alex asked what it did and how it could take pictures. The children had already convinced their grandmother to pick up an international data plan for their cell phones and tablets so they could send information back to their friends on Twitter, Skype, and Snapchat. They had even talked her into getting unlimited minutes. G-Mom had a problem saying no to her two grandchildren. She knew she spoiled them but felt they deserved some of the better things in life, along with the life lessons she was preparing them to face in the future.

G-Mom still did not understand why a twelve-year-old and a ten-year-old had cell phones in the first place, even though she had purchased them for June and Alex. G-Mom grew up in the nontechnology age, but her grandchildren taught her how to use her iPhone and iPad. June and Alex would sometimes tell their friends about their grandmother and referred to her as the "techie grandmother."

The pilot came over the loudspeaker and announced that the flight would be thirteen hours. June and her brother wondered what they could do on an airplane strapped in their seats for thirteen hours. June thought surely they would be able to walk around. As soon as she thought about walking around, a flight attendant came to explain what to expect on the flight and asked what she wanted to drink. June told the flight attendant that she did not have any money for a drink. The flight attendant smiled and said, "You are sitting in first class, my dear, and everything on this flight is free for you, your brother, and your grandmother in the first-class cabin."

Alex's eyes got gigantic, and he displayed the greatest smile that G-Mom had ever seen. Then he asked the flight attendant very sincerely, "What is first class?"

With that question, she assumed that this was their first airplane ride. The flight attendant smiled and told him that she wished she had a grandmother like he had. Most children sat in economy seats on international flights.

June looked at her brother and exclaimed, "Didn't I tell you that's the way G-Mom rolls? Nothing but the best."

The first-class seats could recline back into a bed. June, her brother, and G-Mom had their personal TV monitors, their personal earphones, and their e-book and audio selections if they wanted to read the latest books. The lineup of movies that they could watch was more than June could grasp. The coolest thing of all was the buttons they could push to summon the beautiful woman who served them. Each button was matched to their fingerprint, which June loved. She decided to test using her fingerprint on every single button. Her brother was more interested in tracking the plane route, distance, speed, and altitude on his monitor. June immediately knew that they would not be bored on the flight, as it was just like being home in G-Mom's living room.

G-Mom had a big globe mounted on a table in her living room where she marked every place she traveled. June was looking forward to adding her color dots to her own globe when she returned from this trip. First class even had plush stuffed animals for children to hold when they were about to fall asleep or had to face fear in the sky. June chose an alligator, and Alex chose a tiger.

G-Mom lay back and closed her eyes, thinking about what they would do when the plane landed, as the children were very busy in their seats.

She hoped the tour guide would be at the airport to greet them.

She hoped all of their luggage would arrive with them.

She hoped the weather would be pleasant for the entire trip.

She hoped the children would enjoy the journey.

She hoped her daughter back home would not worry too much about the children.

She hoped she had exchanged enough money from U.S. dollars to euros.

She hoped they would not fly in bad weather that would frighten the children.

She hoped the entire flight would be quite and that they would have a smooth landing.

She hoped, most of all that Lady Bird would still be breathing when they returned.

She secretly said a silent prayer and asked God to take over flying the airplane so that she would not have to worry. Then she said aloud, "Thank you."

June stood up and asked G-Mom who she had been talking to a few minutes earlier. G-Mom looked into June's eyes and told her she was talking to her secret partner. June immediately knew whom she meant because G-Mom talked about her secret partner all the time after leaving church back home or when something was troubling her.

The plane ride was uneventful except for one instance when they hit some dreadful weather. The pilot came over the speaker and asked them to fasten their seat belts. The airplane started to bounce and rock as if it were a softball flying through the air with no aim or direction. It only lasted about a minute but seemed like an eternity to the children. Alex was very brave and did not cry. June, however, was so scared she wet her pants but would not tell G-Mom.

After the turbulence had subsided, the children watched movies, read e-books, and ate all kinds of good food. June and her brother were fascinated by the warm towels they received to wash their faces and hands and the never-ending snack trays that the flight attendant left for them. G-Mom watched the excitement of both children throughout the flight.

G-Mom had to remind the children to get up and walk around and to drink plenty of water to keep them hydrated. June and Alex wanted to see what the flight attendant meant about economy seats, so they slipped from the front of the plane to the back of the aircraft. But first, June made a pit stop to change her underwear. When they returned, June's brother said very loudly that the people in the back of the plane did not get the goodies they had and did not have a bathroom as nice as their bathroom. G-Mom put her hand over his mouth and told him to be quiet. June wanted to know how she and her brother got seats nicer than others in the back section of the plane. G-Mom took advantage of this question to teach the children the value of an education and the many ways to become educated. She explained that bringing them on the trip was part of her way of educating them. She asked both to write in their iPad journals what they had learned from the time they boarded the airplane.

G-Mom did not realize that it would take three hours for them to make notes in their journals. She wondered what they could write for three hours. G-Mom glanced over to see if June and Alex were asleep because they were so quiet. It was a good exercise because it kept them both occupied and in their seats for a while. June wrote about how much she missed Lady Bird, while Alex wrote about how much he worried about what was going on with Lady Bird back home. G-Mom's energy level was waning as she tried to keep up with the two. She was anxious to read the journals when they arrived at the hotel. She quietly reminded herself to use the journal-writing technique throughout the trip when she needed to recharge her battery.

Another Crack

THE POWER OF SILENCE

If you stay silent long enough, you can hear things coming before they arrive.

Charles de Gaulle once said, "Silence is the ultimate weapon of power."

Kids know how to use it well.

Chapter 3

YOUTH TRUMPS WISDOM

The three were met at baggage claim at Munich by a beautiful young lady holding a sign with the tour name on it. June and Alex looked at their name tags to see if the sign matched their tour company name. It did!

There were about forty people in the group, but June and her brother were the only children. June knew that her brother was a charmer and couldn't wait to see how he would get his way with the grown-ups in the group. Alex started right away with the tour guide telling her how beautiful her uniform was and how he loved her backpack. She said he was such a cutie. June rolled her eyes at her brother and smiled. After all, she would be the recipient too of the many things she knew would come their way throughout the trip as a result of her brother's charm. The tour guide spoke several languages. She dressed slightly different from the group always wearing a straw hat. Each day, she changed the color of her hat and her matching socks.

They checked into the first hotel on the itinerary and got a good night's sleep. Upon waking the next morning, both children ran to the window to see what was outside because it had been dark when they had arrived the evening before. G-Mom told them to get dressed to eat breakfast early so that they could get a good seat on the tour bus.

The children had never seen a breakfast like the one the hotel had prepared. They did like the bread, juice, and butter—the only food that was familiar to them but not the other food. The other members of the group seemed to enjoy their breakfast immensely. Alex held up a tomato and a slice of plantain and asked if it was a breakfast food. The tour guide assured him it was delicious, but Alex did not trust her judgment yet, so he slipped it into his pocket. He planned to use it later in the trip to trade with the tour guide for something else he might want to do that was not on the itinerary.

As the group boarded the luxury bus to start their trip through Europe, G-Mom positioned herself so that she could watch the children, look out the window at the scenery, and at the same time freely communicate with the adults. When the bus pulled out to get on the Autobahn, a road where cars did not have speed limits, the tour guide started talking about where they were going for the day and what they could expect to see. June went to the back of the bus to inspect the bathroom. June's brother was fixated on the highway with no speed limits and no stoplights, imagining the speed of movement. While returning from the bathroom, June was looking at all the *old people*, as she thought of them, on the bus, wondering what they would have to talk about with children their age.

An engaging member of the tour wore hearing aids, thick glasses, and stood about five feet tall. He was a quiet man who kept mostly to himself. Often, the children watched him looking over the rim of his glasses. He wore a vest jacket that had many pockets each stuffed with bulging objects. His hair had turned completely gray, and he wore it in a ponytail. Alex told June the ponytail made the man feel taller than he was. When he smiled, his face made a funny twist. June and Alex knew they needed to keep a close eye on him.

The lady who jumped on the front seat of the bus with the long salt and pepper color hair hanging down her back kept her eye on the children. She talked non-stop about nothing yet captured the attention of fellow tourists. For someone who talked so much, she had two missing front teeth. Every time she opened her mouth, June and Alex would cover their face and laugh. The children admitted that she could be a fun person to be around. Her jokes were clean and funny, and she had a personality like a fuzzy bear.

One of the tourist made friends with G-Mom as soon as they landed at the airport. Her name was Kia. Kia went with G-Mom on another tour. They hugged each other and exchanged cell phone numbers. Kia packed enough snacks to feed everyone on the tour. She never missed an opportunity to share recipes with her fellow bus mates. Kia loved to sing often leading the group in song as they traveled. G-Mom remembered that Kia always slept with one eye open and one eye closed. So, G-Mom whispered to Kia, "Help me to keep a look at the children without them knowing you are watching."

Kia replied, "You know these kids are just like they are my own. I am so happy to be able to meet them in person. You have talked so much about both Alex and June. They are as adorable as you described. I suspect this is going to be a trip that goes down in history as one of our best tours due to the presence of these energetic little munchkins."

On the first forty-five-minute bus trip, G-Mom noticed the leaves on the trees were so beautiful—red, yellow, orange, brown, an array of colors and breathtaking to look at from her window, as opposed to the open road. They saw graffiti on bridges that looked like a rainbow of colors, nothing like the graffiti back home; artwork on small cars; and big transport trucks with bright colors and lovely scenes. To keep the children in their seats, G-Mom suggested games for them to play to learn about the surroundings.

June and Alex played the *color* game to see who could find a car that matched the color of the leaves on the trees. They sat on opposite sides of the bus. They got so loud G-Mom thought they would disturb the other travelers. The trees had tall, shaped branches adorned by a river of colors. The design of the trees was something the children had not seen before. Being so high up on the mountain road, the kids could look down through the overcast skies at the tops of the trees, as well as rooftops made of red, yellow, and green wood or bricks.

When the children saw something unique, they would yell, "Look!" and cameras would start snapping. The tour guide announced that she had two wonderful new helpers on the bus who could see beauty and uniqueness through a lens that most grown-ups did not use. G-Mom told the children that trees were God's way of showing He was the designer of nature. Alex chimed in and said the water running down the mountain was God's tears being used to exhibit the beauty of rainfall. June's brother won the game. He found twenty colors while June only found twelve. June and Alex did not know the dark secrets scattered over the bus that would surface later in the day.

The next game they played was selecting the most distinctive transport trucks while traveling throughout Austria. The bus passed hundreds of trucks at truck stops and on the road. The children had never seen so many trucks that had such lovely scenes painted on the sides on their trips in the States, like they saw on this journey. They saw trucks with big apples, a huge sunshine face, big patches of strawberries, a farm brought to life with cows and chickens, a rainbow of colors on one truck, and even one with a racetrack showing an array of cars floating over mountains and around curves. The children's enthusiasm overflowed into the adults, who joined in the game rather than sleep. The tour guide explained that there were so many trucks at the truck stop because the truckers could not drive on the Autobahn on Sunday, as this was family time.

At the next rest stop, June announced that she had seen twenty different trucks and thought she had won the game. An elderly ponytail gentleman, who looked to June and her brother to be one hundred years old, raised his hand and said, "Oh no, I beat you. I saw twenty-five trucks, and I've got the pictures on my camera to prove it."

The other bus passengers burst out with laughter and applause. June looked at him in amazement but did not dare disrespect the elderly. As fast as the bus was traveling, she wondered how he could see the paintings on so many more trucks than she did. Surely his glasses had a telescope or video camera attached to them. She thought the game was just between her and her brother. So, she allowed him to take credit for the win, joining in the clapping. G-Mom made a note to discuss later with June the impact of her enthusiasm on the elderly man and what joy she had brought into his trip. Alex and June took advantage of the pit stop. They ran from truck to truck to get a better look at the paintings. Alex, of course, decided right then and there that he was going to be an artist when he grew up so that he could paint on trucks.

When it was time for the bus to leave, the tour guide noticed that June and Alex were missing. Panic gripped G-Mom in the stomach. How could she lose the kids at the first stop? Everyone left the bus and immediately started looking for the kids. After a few minutes,

June and Alex popped out from behind one of the big trucks, waving and smiling. The tour guide screamed at both of the children, as she was also frightened that she had lost the children in a foreign country. Knowing they were in serious trouble, Alex pulled out the breakfast plantain and tomato and offered it to the tour guide as a peace offering. It was done with so much innocence and charm that everyone relaxed and started laughing. The "ole folks" returned to the bus. June whispered in Alex's ear to let him know they were still in big-time trouble with G-Mom. They decided it would be safer to sit in the seat with the one-hundred-year-old man rather than in their own seats. They figured G-Mom would not say anything that way.

"Studying geography on vacation? Who does that?" June and her brother could not understand why the next game G-Mom selected was to read license plates on cars. G-Mom was furious with the kids so she decided to choose a game she knew they would not like.

The day before, the tour guide had explained that the first two letters on the license plates of cars signaled the country where the driver might live. So, G-Mom had the children take out their journals and for thirty minutes, write down the first two letters that they saw on the license plates of cars as the group traveled on the luxury bus to Switzerland. The cars were moving as fast as the bus, so the children had to have good eye-hand coordination and be fast to capture the license plates. Before they started, the children announced what they had been told to do and glanced over at the elderly gentleman to see if he had taken out a pad to write on also. The children wrote down these letters: ZI, NL, GRU, DWL, W, KA, HP, TR, ME, HD, HP, F, H, DA, HN, MZ, MA, GG, ZW, AZ WW, AM BG, AKA, WI, AB, and OF. After thirty minutes, the children could do whatever they wanted to do within reason. Both kids were very competitive and knew silence was the main dish for the rest of the trip.

At the end of the day's bus ride, June and Alex decided to take a nap before going for dinner. Their eyes were slowly closing when Alex heard a knock on the door. G-Mom opened the door to see three ladies from the group standing there. G-Mom invited the women into her hotel room. The girls were wearing big smiles on their faces. The leader, with the missing two front teeth, said they wanted to compare their license plate records with the children's. The women started giggling and recited what they had written. Then they asked the children to compare with their lists. G-Mom pulled out the map of Europe and invited the women to go to dinner later with her and her grandchildren so that they could identify each country.

After finishing dinner, the group gathered around the table to start their tasks, not realizing that a crowd had gathered to help with the puzzles. Once again, the children had brought excitement and joy into the lives of more group members by playing a game of geography.

The children soon realized that their grandmother was very smart to use education in all of the games while building friendships and relationships that would last a lifetime. Everyone was a winner in this match.

When traveling in the United States on road trips, June and her brother also played the license-plate game. They put colored dots on the map for every state from which they had identified cars. At the end of each trip, G-Mom gave the winner a bonus of ice cream every weekend for a month. The race was always competitive between the children. G-Mom was quite the witty grandmother. She never stopped teaching. She always said, "Learning is a journey. Have fun while traveling and learn at the same time." She helped the children choose activities that were a learning experience. The children often wondered what was running around in her silver head. Sometimes, June and her brother played guessing games to identify the objects she would focus on for the next road trip. They learned to enjoy traveling with her because for an *old person*, she made annoying things fresh and time passed quickly with her. The ice cream bonuses were just incentives that they didn't have to have but enjoyed nevertheless.

As they boarded the next morning, June looked around the bus several times and whispered in Alex's ear, "There are still no other children on this bus. These people are older than G-Mom, and she is eighty years old."

Alex started laughing uncontrollably. He then slowly looked around as if he was searching to find at least one other child in the group. When he was sure there were no other kids, he then whispered to June, "Leave it to me. I got this! Being the only children in a group of old people is so great. As I told you before, I will charm their pants off. Just follow my lead."

Alex boarded the bus, wearing a gigantic smile, and handed out candy sticks to all the passengers. He would bow like a gentleman and then say something really nice about how he liked the person's hat, shoes, perfume or cologne, or bags. He made his way to his seat, still smiling, and gave June a high five.

Crack 3

THE POWER OF LAUGHTER

Kids say the "darndest" things.
Someone once said, "Old people are little kids in disguise."

*Dogs are perfect soldiers; wags, paws, and
licks are their arsenal of power weapons.
Kids are innocent angels; smiles, hugs, antics, and
dancing eyes are their stockpile of power weapons.*

Chapter 4

THE SHADOW OF REVERSE LENS

One of her most exciting games occurred while riding the luxury bus on day 4 of the trip. She called it the "trash game." She had the children look out the window of the bus to see what kind of trash people had on the dash, seats, and back window of their cars. Most of the cars were tiny compared to the majority of U.S. cars. It was, therefore, a clear view from the tall bus down into the cars. Who could come up with such an unusual game for a ten-year-old other than G-Mom? The children had no idea what they would gain from this little game but were willing to give it a try just to see what would occur. Again, they looked over at the elderly man to see what he was doing. He appeared to be fast asleep until he heard June tell her brother to come over to her side of the bus to see the puppies in the little red convertible. Looking at the puppies in the red convertible, many of the travelers commented on the cute animals. The elderly gentleman quickly rose up and took a peek out the window, as his seat was in front of June's place. The old man listened for a few minutes to learn the object of this game.

What do you think G-Mom wanted the children to learn from this match? Keep reading. Alex said no one would guess in a million years what G-Mom wanted them to learn. The elderly gentleman chimed in and said, "Not in a trillion years." Another passenger said there was nothing to gain but a lot to see. Another added that the children knew G-Mom better than anyone, and they could not wait to see what she would teach them from this game. So the observation began with more than ten people watching out the windows to see what they could see in the cars below them. They were alternating looking at cars and the countryside because they did not want to miss anything. The Black Forest had tall green fir trees with orange and yellow trees mingled in, projecting the picturesque forest as a warm and relaxing place to explore. It looked like magic in Wonderland, which the elderly man captured on his camera.

The conversation about trash in cars overpowered the tour guide's explanations of what they were passing through. She finally realized the children were a plus for her and was so good at entertaining. She learned when to chime in to the passengers' conversations to convey her facts about the countryside.

Because the cars were moving so fast, June realized that she could not see every car. The vehicles were so interesting that she took out her journal and started writing what she had observed in the cars. She suggested that her brother do the same.

Car 1—piles of candy wrappers on the front dash and all kinds of crushed drink cans in the back window
Car 2—backseats spread with popcorn and empty popcorn boxes
Car 3—three dogs in the front and four dogs in the back with a small boy squeezed in the middle of the dogs

> Car 4—a tiny smart car with two seats and three adults cramped in the front seats, too funny!
> Car 5—a red van with three cell phones on the front dashboard, an active iPad on the front seat, a TV playing a cartoon, and the driver with a cell phone up to her ear
> Car 6—backseat filled with old newspapers while the front passenger seat seemed filled with old magazines, no way could a person sit on those seats
> Car 7—thousands of empty coffee cups in the front seat with fast-food restaurant burger wrappers and a beautiful pink stuffed teddy bear sitting on top of the pile of junk

Suddenly, June realized car 7 was a police vehicle and called her brother over to take a look. The elderly gentlemen took a picture. June continued her list.

> Car 8—looks like about ten kids packed inside, each holding other kids that look like they were from many different kinds of families

After June had finished writing, she moved from seat to seat to hear what others were seeing. She realized that adults did not see the same kinds of things that she saw. It made her wonder what her brother was seeing in his cars, since he rarely saw things the same way she did. After she had finished writing and listening to the adults on her side of the bus, June moved over to her brother's side of the bus and asked what he had seen. She read his list.

> Car 1—a passenger working on his iPad in his lap with his feet propped on the dashboard

> Car 2—backseat with three Rollerblades of various colors, front panel had honey buns spread out as if they were using the dashboard as an oven or warmer
> Car 3—stacks of comic books in backseat, newspapers in front seat
> Car 4—chewing gum stuck on front dashboard
> Car 5—a female in the backseat is changing clothes from business suit to jogging suit, tossing clothes in the front seat of the car

Her brother's sheepish smile told her how much he enjoyed watching this car. Then the one-hundred-year-old man gave a sneaky grin and said her underclothes were "hot red."

"Ugh!" June thought and continued reading.

> Car 6—a goat in the lap of a woman, who has a bottle and is feeding the goat
> Car 7—a bicycle in the backseat with two children cramped close to the door
> Car 8—a cage in the backseat that looks like it has chickens inside
> Car 9—what appears to be a boy who looks to be my age, driving the car with two grown-ups in the backseat
> Car 10—a clean car with a driver, nothing on the seats or dash

Finally, G-Mom came to sit on the seat with June and had her brother sit immediately opposite her so that she could talk to the children at the same time. The other participants asked G-Mom to wait until they got to the hotel so that they could share what they had seen.

Truthfully, they wanted to hear what G-Mom would teach the children from this exercise.

The old man was so interested that he joined the group for dinner for the first time since the trip started. He did not eat in his room that night. No one knew that he was listening to June when she saw a car of interest, and then he would take a picture. Alex was jealous that his sister had evidence through the old man's pictures and he did not. The group spent hours laughing and sharing what they had seen on the bus ride that day while G-Mom mentally took notes of what she wanted to summarize later.

Nothing the children saw surprised their granny, as she had seen it all before. Many of the cars were a surprise for June and Alex and a few of the others in the tour group. G-Mom was not interested in what the children saw so much as what they thought of the kind of clutter, the volume of clutter, and the kind of people who had it. G-Mom was hoping that the children would pick up on sanitation and safety issues from this exercise. Of course, the kids were more excited about the descriptions and comparing what they had seen. June enjoyed playing the game even though at first she thought it would be boring.

G-Mom had a lesson in all of the fun games she had the children playing. June said she thought G-Mom wanted them to learn to see what others took for granted and to think about situations in an entirely different way. Alex thought G-Mom was just trying to keep them busy. The elderly man's interpretation was so on target with what G-Mom wanted the children to learn. He talked about trusting our instincts, respecting the wisdom of the old, and embellishing faith. He said, "Colors bring joy, peace, and warmth into the heart and mind if we look at them in a different way and accept the delivery, as colors mixed can create unimaginable beauty like the forest and the trucks."

G-Mom had the children play games the first five days to get their minds off home and to establish new relationships for the remainder of the trip. G-Mom wanted the kids to stop thinking so much about what Lady Bird might be doing, even though she knew Lady Bird would sit at the door, waiting for June's return. She probably would eat very little.

The tour guide did not want this part to end, as the group so enjoyed interacting with the children. Most of the people in the group were over eighty years old, and they were from all over the United States. The children were having the best time of their young lives. At the end of the day, both kids would give G-Mom a big hug and tell her how much they loved her.

June and Alex were having so much fun that they had not used the cell phones, their e-readers, or their iPads, except to journal. They had not even turned the TV on since they arrived. G-Mom was a little worried at the beginning of the trip when she realized her grandchildren would be the only children on the tour. But after day four, she decided it was one of the best decisions she had made in a long time.

June and Alex were having fun and learning so many new things that they would not have the opportunity to learn had they taken another trip in the States. They saw things through reverse lens. The worries G-Mom had inside her head gradually began to go away.

During days five through twelve, everyone so enjoyed the winding roads through the trees and the snowcapped mountains. Although the bus driver had taken the group in many areas of the country, nothing was more beautiful than the altitude snow on the top of mountains flowing slowly down the incline over the tree tops. The air seemed sprinkled with beautiful snowflakes. There were hills covered with white snow too but no snow on the roads since it was summer. Roads had steep curves, and big trucks traveled on the slippery surfaces. The children were allowed to sit in the front seat so they could see everything. It was very scary when they looked down to see the tops of the trees through snow-covered valleys. White snow blanketed the land to the horizon as far as the eye could see. Trees draped in white snowflakes lit up like Christmas trees in the sunlight. June and Alex wanted the bus to stop so they could get out to make a snowman or throw snowballs at each other. But the driver explained that it was too dangerous to stop and impossible to trek up the mountain to get near the snow.

There were streams of water running down the mountains that looked like sparkles in the night sky. The children were fascinated to see trees growing out of the sides of mountains and wondered how they kept from falling. Rock formations captured their imagination with colors and shapes like they had never seen. Europe's largest waterfall sprayed water over their toes as they looked out over the streams of water flowing over the dam. The children's little feet had to be wrapped in foot warmers when they returned to the bus after testing the water at the bottom of the waterfall.

There were big, empty castles with walls covered in beautiful pictures and elaborate sparkling chandeliers. Some of the images were of men dressed in funny-looking clothes. The group did not like all of the stairs to climb to reach the third floor to see where the prince slept and ate, but the children ran up the stairs, skipping several steps at a time. June and Alex lay on the floor in the middle of the rotunda, looking up at the artwork on the ceiling. Alex was even more determined to become an artist.

The tour guide made a stop at a monastery, where June and Alex saw books that were over two hundred years old. Books covered walls as far as the eye could see. They could not touch the books, which was OK with Alex since he was not too keen on reading.

Riding in one of the world's largest Ferris wheels had proven to be what the children needed to culminate their day-twelve trip. On the last night, the children had dinner with the friends they had made on the journey inside the Ferris wheel. Eating pizza miles up in the sky while looking down at the people who looked like little rats running around made the children laugh. Both children smiled at their one-hundred-year-old friend because he finally admitted he was afraid of heights. They held his hand, walked to the windows, and convinced him to look down at the people below. He felt at ease with the two children holding his hand.

The trip back to the United States was uneventful. June and Alex looked forward to flying first class and could not wait to get home to tell their mother, stepfather, and new stepsisters and stepbrothers all about the fantastic fifteen days they had spent in Europe. June knew that Lady Bird would be waiting for her at the front door. It was too much to expect that her mother would bring Lady Bird to the airport to meet them.

Another Crack

THE POWER OF COMPANIONSHIP

Ben Williams once said, "There is no psychiatrist in the world like a puppy licking your face."
Too often, we underestimate the *power* of a touch, a silent hug, a gentle bark, a listening ear, an honest nudge, or the smallest act of caring, all of which have the potential to turn a life around.

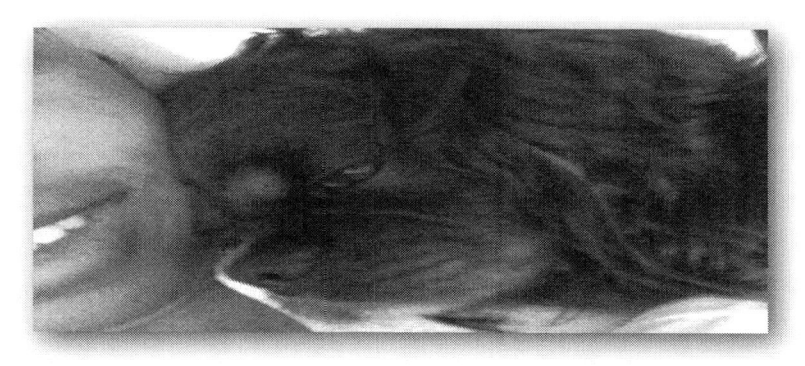

*Dogs are perfect soldiers; wags, paws, and
licks are their arsenal of power weapons.
Kids are innocent angels; smiles, hugs, antics, and
dancing eyes are their stockpile of power weapons.*

Chapter 5

BACK HOME TO SMALL TOWN, USA

Upon returning from their vacation, June and Alex spent the concluding part of the summer at home, playing with the neighborhood children. G-Mom went back to her home to get some much-needed rest. She called the children once a week to check on them.

Every year, G-Mom would send money for the children to go shopping for school clothes and school supplies. Sending shopping money could not happen this year. So, G-Mom donated her time and money to her favorite children's charity. As long as G-Mom kept busy, she did not have to worry about the stinging pains in her back or the fact that she never got hungry. When the children would call and ask how she was doing, G-Mom would always say, "OK." She didn't dare burden the children with how she had slowed down. Instead of walking five miles per day, she was now walking three and sometimes not at all.

The doctor was not very concerned about her symptoms. He attributed her pains to old age. That, of course, was the wrong thing to say to G-Mom, a woman who had built her life upon truth, integrity, honesty, and trust. She no longer trusted her doctor, as she knew her symptoms were not from old age. She listened to her body, which spoke to her through symptoms. She was notorious for treating herself using herbal medicine.

Six months after their incredible, fun-filled trip to Europe, June called G-Mom and told her that she was not feeling well. June trusted G-Mom to talk to about her health because she knew she ran a hospital. G-Mom called her daughter and asked her if June was feeling sick. Amy said, "June complains about everything."

G-Mom, however, felt that this was not just a minor complaint. She decided to call Alex to see if he would mention anything about changes in June's behavior. She approached the conversation by asking what Lady Bird was up to these days. Alex told her that Lady Bird followed June carefully, stayed by her door when she was trying to study, and had started sleeping on the foot of her bed. Alex instructed G-Mom not to tell his mom that Lady Bird was sleeping in the bed. Alex also said he was making better grades than June. With that statement, G-Mom saw a warning flag go up.

A week later, June called again, explaining that she was still not feeling well. G-Mom called June's school and spoke with several of her teachers, who conveyed the changes they had noticed in June's physical appearance and her attention span in the classroom. June was not doing as well in school. The teachers felt comfortable talking with G-Mom because they were aware of the family dynamics.

G-Mom told June she was taking a plane the next day to come and see her. June instantly thought she felt better after talking with G-Mom. When G-Mom arrived, she took one look at June and knew something was terribly wrong—something that herbal medicine could not fix; nor would a trip to the bathroom to do number two help. She did not advocate herbal medicine for children. June had lost weight and looked very pale. Her beautiful smile had faded into an eerie stare. Her spontaneity had disappeared. She was unable to string words together to form a complete sentence. It appeared as if she were looking straight through G-Mom, like she did not recognize her.

    G-Mom made an appointment for June to see the doctor the next day after school. She feared the worst, but Amy continued saying she did not think anything was wrong. Her daughter apparently was too close to notice the changes G-Mom had, or else she was oblivious to her immediate surroundings. The doctor ran test after test but could not pinpoint what was wrong even though she said the symptoms mimicked a rare form of cancer. She was not sure enough to make a final diagnosis and wanted to get a second opinion. The doctor sent June to a hospital that had a reputation and diagnostic equipment that many smaller facilities did not have. After two more days of testing, the world as they knew it was no more. June's diagnosis came back with stage 3 of a very rare form of brain cancer.

    The doctor explained the prognosis and treatment modalities but said there were no promises she could make for an immediate cure or that they could stop the spread into other vital organs. The prognosis is grave. She explained that June would have to be hospitalized immediately to continue tests and to come up with an aggressive treatment plan. G-Mom knew that Amy should tell June how sick she was, but she also knew her daughter was falling apart right before her eyes. June, her best friend, and only granddaughter were on a collision course. G-Mom wondered about June's school and how her teachers would take the news when she called to tell them.

Crack 5 The most important code

THE POWER OF GRANDMA'S LOVE

Love supersedes all.
People protect the strangest of species and creatures
(dogs and other kids) as if they birthed them.

*Dogs are perfect soldiers; wags, paws, and
licks are their arsenal of power weapons.
Kids are innocent angels; smiles, hugs, antics, and
dancing eyes are their stockpile of power weapons.*

Chapter 6

TRUTH COLLIDES WITH REALITY

Most parents tend to go into a state of denial or a state of blaming. June's mom, Amy, went into a rage. She said if she had not allowed June to go on the trip to Europe, this might not have happened. She blamed June for not telling her sooner that she wasn't feeling well. June was too afraid to say anything to her mother. Amy blamed Alex for not noticing that something was wrong with his sister. She approached her neighbor and asked June's friend, Kayla, why she had not told her that June was failing in class. Amy even accused the church! She told the doctor that evidently she had made a mistake and that June needed to be tested by someone more competent than she was. It was not unusual for the doctor to hear these types of accusations from parents when delivering bad news about their child. Amy insisted on taking June to another city to have the test done there because she did not trust this doctor. G-Mom allowed Amy to calm down somewhat and told her to go home and wait until she had finished talking with all the doctors.

June had an evaluation in the best cancer hospital in the state. People from all over the world came to this hospital for diagnosis and treatment. To appease her daughter, G-Mom had the doctor send all lab results and X-rays to another expert of Amy's choice, preferably out of the state, for a second opinion with an expedited rush on the request. The second opinion came in within twenty-four hours with the same diagnosis. This little girl, who had had the time of her life six months ago, was about to enter an incredible journey through a tunnel of darkness.

Upon learning that she was very sick and would have to be in the hospital for a long time, June's first question was "Will G-Mom stay with me?"

Of course, Amy went into another jealous rage because June did not ask for her to stay with her. G-Mom took her daughter aside and explained that this was not a time for anger but a time to come together as one to get through a difficult time. She further explained that blame was as toxic as guilt.

June had an uncanny ability to read body language very well. She also picked up on tones in voices as well as interactions between parties. June was a smart little girl who sometimes had to be the grown-up instead of the child. G-Mom asked Amy if she wanted her to stay to help get her through this difficult period. With hesitation, Amy said she did until she figured out what to do next. G-Mom said she would stay with June while her daughter went home to tell the family what was going on.

Sitting close to June's bed, the doctor explained the disease in such a way that did not frighten June. She held June's hand the entire time she was speaking to her. The explanation made June very comfortable with the doctor, and June knew she could trust this doctor. She was also brave because G-Mom was in the room with her, and she knew G-Mom would not let them do anything to her that was not the right thing to do. When the doctor left the room, June jokingly told G-Mom that the crazy disease inside her body needed a name. She gave it the name *Noma* since the physician used the word *carcinoma*. June also told G-Mom that the way the doctor explained the condition sounded like Noma had set up a tree house in her body and that Noma would be ingenious. She said they had to learn how to outsmart Noma and close all exit points out of the tree house. Based on what the doctor had said, June suspected that Noma had about eleven ways to enter other parts of the body and three escape routes.

G-Mom looked at June in sheer amazement, thinking how smart this ten-year-old must be to be able to understand what was going on inside herself so vividly. June's explanation painted a clearer picture for G-Mom as well.

Fear had not entered June's mind yet. Nor had June grasped how bad the side effects from the treatments she would soon need would be. June was glad that someone had finally listened to her when she said she was not feeling well. Even though the grown-ups did not listen, June was confident that Lady Bird understood. Nevertheless, G-Mom was convinced that this little girl was mentally strong enough to withstand anything.

Little did G-Mom know that the trip they had just taken through Europe would help June to get through the tough times ahead. G-Mom decided to call her new friends from the Europe trip to let them know about June's illness. All were devastated, including the tour guide, the bus driver, and the one-hundred-year-old man, who was not actually that old, though through the children's eyes, he appeared to be. They exaggerated years. Oh how the adults had enjoyed the tour with June and Alex! It had been one of the best tours they had had in such a long time. They said the children made them feel young. They questioned how something like this could happen to such a little angel. G-Mom assured them that she would keep in touch as June went through this journey.

The doctor decided that since June was in stage three, she needed to start aggressive treatment. She decided on a combination chemotherapy and radiation treatment.

Crack 6

THE POWER OF BODY LANGUAGE

Roving eyes are worth a thousand words.

A dog can express more with his tail in minutes than his owner can express with his tongue in hours.

—*Anonymous*

Chapter 7

JUNE FINDS INSPIRATION

JUNE'S STORY IN HER OWN WORDS

Hey, everyone, I have a rare form of cancer running around in my head. Being in my hospital room gives me lots of alone time to think. Sometimes, I am scared. Sometimes, I am hopeful. Most times, I am thankful. There are times when I get very lonely. There are times when I ask, "Why Me?" There are times when I look at other children in this hospital and don't think about what is going on with me because they are so much worse off than I am. There are times when I cry myself to sleep because I want to see my brother and my dog, Lady Bird. There are even times when I just don't want to wake up and get out of bed. I am feeling like I am going into a depression and the worst kind of pity party. I am starting to act just like my mom. If someone said, "Good morning," I might say, "What is good about it?" rather than saying, "You have a happy day," or "Happy Monday to you."

Because I have so much time alone to think, I create make-believe friends. When it is time to take chemotherapy, I order my favorite juice or pop flavors. I named the chemotherapy treatment my friend

Chemo. There is a technician who comes to my room daily to make changes to the medication bags hanging above my head. He's one of my favorite technicians. He's always doing something to make me smile. One day, he put food coloring in my drip to turn the drip to my favorite color, pink. I was overjoyed and bursting with happiness the whole day. He made me swear not to tell because he was afraid he would get into trouble.

I have another friend whom I see three times per week. Rad is my radiation treatment. When it is time to take treatments, I call this treatment my friend Rad. When they roll me down to have the gigantic machine ease over my body, I often tell Rad to make sure he pumps neon so I will glow in the dark, as I love an assortment of colors. Sometimes, I try to bargain with Rad but can never get him to play with me my way. Once I told him beef jerky would be nice, but Rad did not have a sense of humor.

Some of the other kids on my ward take experimental drugs, and I refer to this treatment as my friend Ed. Chemo, Rad, and ED are my friends because these friends work very hard with other kids and me to make us better.

I did not tell any of my family about the talks because since I have a brain condition someone may think I am crazy. I even came up with two superheroes. One is my doctor, and I call her General Treehouse. The other is a friend I talk with when I need to feel something other than pain. I call him Captain Jeff. My most important hero of all time is my grandmother; I can always count on her to lift my spirits. Whom do you have? Yours maybe your mother and father, a nurse, or a friend, but for me, it's my grandmother. As a result of my journey, I have aged in wisdom beyond that of a ten-year-old.

So, before I share my story with you, I have a special message for my teachers.

JUNE THE PRUNE AND LADY BIRD

To All My Teachers,

I will come back to school someday, and I hope by reading my story, you will have a better understanding of how I coped with this thing and what you need to do to help other children in your classroom faced with special needs or circumstances beyond their control. Do not show pity; show love and understanding. As my grandmother told me, I want the same thing from you as any other child in your classroom. Teach me to be extraordinary by using those traits that are unique to me. Hold me to the same high expectations that you have for any other child. Don't look at me as a sick child, but see me as a blessed child. My new team-Rad, Chemo, General Treehouse, Captain Jeff, and my grandmother (G-Mom)-will teach me while I am absent from your classroom. I have my iPad that G-Mom bought me. If you want to Skype the difficult lessons to me, my grandmother, who was once a college professor, can act as my bedside teacher when I need an explanation or can turn me off Skype when I am getting too exhausted. Don't worry; though I will fall behind slightly, when I return, I will catch up quickly. Tell all my classmates to pay me a visit sometime if the doctors allow it. Then, they can tell me all about the things I am missing. Please explain to them about my appearance and what to expect when they see me so they won't be shocked. My head is bald. Tell them that I am fragile and possibly wobbly from loss of strength. I am still June, but I look like a prune. I believe in you and hope you can do this for me.

Happy Cheers,
June the Prune

Another Crack

THE POWER OF POSITIVE THINKING

Out-of-control emotions make smart people stupid.

*Expose yourself to your deepest fear;
after that, fear has no power.*

—J$_{IM}$ M$_{ORRISON}$

Chapter 8

FOOD FROM MARS

My doctor, Dr. Treehouse, strolled into my room and announced that she was going to teach me a lesson in anatomy. I looked at her with a charming smile. She realized she needed to tell me what she meant by *anatomy* first. She discussed everything in doctor language. I did understand some of what she was saying, but she could see that she needed to tell it another way. The doctor used a tree, the same way I did with G-Mom, to explain what was going on inside of me, hence the reason I nicknamed her General Treehouse out of respect. She said I should think of the tree trunk as my waist down, the side branches as my arms, and the treetop as waist up. She began to explain that a foreign substance had entered my body, causing me to stumble, see double, and feel fragile. She showed me a picture of my brain to explain what had changed. She then showed me a picture of a tree pointing out what had occurred.

She told me that was enough for one day and that she would come back the next day to talk more about why I was feeling so ill and losing so much weight. She was right; she had put me into information overload. I understood most of what she had said because of what had been happening to me. I was once an "A" student in my class, but lately, I could not finish my assignments because I did not know what to do next. I didn't want to eat. I didn't listen to my mom, and she thought I was being stubborn and had an attitude. I started to repeat my words when talking. I couldn't remember things. I was falling for no reason but would not let my mom see it. I even initiated fights in class with my friends for no good reason, and my teachers would send me to the principal's office. The principal would send notes home to my mother, and I was yelled at or put on punishment. The sad part was that I did not know what I had done wrong or why I was being punished. I was really scared. That was why I called my grandmother; I knew she would listen and understand how scared I was. Everything the doctor told me made sense—sort of.

Several days later, my doctor made another visit to my room. I asked her where she had been for so long. She took my hand, massaged it, smiled, and said, "My little angel, I will never forget about you."

Her words made me feel better. I told her to explain what she put in the bags hanging over my head that dripped into my body through my arms, through a tube in my stomach, and through tubes in my head and my nose. I had drawn a cool picture to show her what I thought I looked like with all the tubes sticking out of my head and nose. The picture made General Treehouse laugh. She asked if she could keep the image. I looked like an alien from outer space.

General Treehouse wanted to make me laugh too, so she asked me what my favorite food was. I told her several things: chocolate cake, G-Mom's brand of ice cream, pizza, hotdogs, chicken nuggets, and all kinds of juice except apple juice.

General Treehouse said, "I asked about your favorite *food*; that means one item," and laughed.

GRACIE BRADFORD

My doctor told me that the first day she was gone, she ordered the dietitian to prepare my favorite foods to be put into my stomach tube because the doctor needed me to gain some strength fast before she started treatments for what I called "Noma." The dietitian and I bonded on the first visit. She taught me techniques to pretend I was actually eating my favorite chocolate cake. We called it the fabulous, tasteless chocolate cake. Every time she came to my room, I would make a point of requesting food that I thought she would not be able to get. But she always tried. Once I told her that I wanted some black licorice and thought I had her. But the next meal, they delivered pureed licorice that looked like dog poop. Can you believe that?

My doctor knew that I would not be able to eat very much by mouth. I guess I can say she was exceptionally nice today. She then told me she needed to rehydrate me. I asked what she was talking about, as I did not understand the meaning of *hydrate*. She said I needed lots of water for my body to replenish what I am losing.

Finally, with a sad voice, I said to my doctor, "You do know I am only ten years old?"

She smiled and said, "But you are so mature and intelligent for a ten-year-old, considering the kind of cancer you have." She got the point and began breaking the medical terms she used down into what I could understand.

My doctor was about the same height as me. She had lovely long hair, which she wore in a ponytail most of the time. Her face reminded me of the face of a doll that G-Mom bought for me when I was five years old. The doctor's teeth were snow white like the snow my brother and I saw on the mountains of the Alps in Switzerland, and she had blue eyes the color of the waterfalls we saw in Germany. Sometimes I wondered if she was a real doctor. She always wore a white lab coat with pretty, colorful clothes under her white coat that reminded me of the beautiful colors in the trees we saw when we traveled the Autobahn in Austria. I looked at her hands and noticed that she did not wear nail polish. I wondered if she wore makeup, as her face looked so clean and glowing.

When she spoke, she had a slight accent but talked like me most of the time. Her voice was soft and soothing, like some of the music of the songs we heard when we went to a Mozart concert during vacation. Her accent would come when she got annoyed with the nurses about something she had told them to do that she thought they did not do. She had to sit on a tall stool next to my bed to be high enough to talk to me at my eye level. I noticed that she wore black shoes with low heels. Her skin was very soft, like cotton. She reminded me of me, and I thought maybe I was dreaming.

I knew she was real when she said, "Let's talk about your treatment." She asked my parents to come into the room. My mother and stepfather were in the hall, pacing the floor. I told Dr. Treehouse not to start until my grandmother was in the room. G-Mom had told everyone that she was going downstairs to get some hot tea, but I knew she was probably going to a quiet place to have a conversation with the one she calls her "partner." G-Mom is a churchgoing woman and believes strongly in the works of God. When she prays, she always tells my brother and me that prayer is her partner. Alex thought her male friend was her partner.

My doctor asked more questions about my school, what kind of clothes I liked to wear, my favorite colors, my friends, my pets, and my family while we were waiting for G-Mom to return to my room. Of course, I talked the whole time about my dog, Lady Bird. She shared stories about what made her become a doctor and told us a little about her family. I think she was trying to get to know me better or make me feel at ease.

After about ten minutes, G-Mom returned to the waiting area, and my brother, Alex, told her that I insisted she be in the room when the doctor explained my remaining treatment plan. My brother and G-Mom entered the room with sad faces. I tried to tell a joke to lighten up the atmosphere, but it did not work. It was time to face a "moment of truth," as G-Mom often said.

Chapter 9

CHEMO AND RAD PARTNERSHIP

The doctor told us that her goal was to shrink the size of the mass in my head, which was pushing against an area that controlled some of my mental and physical functions while at the same time reduce side effects and maintain my quality of life during and after the treatments. She said that surgery was not an option that she wanted to take at this time. I was so glad to hear that they were not going to shave my hair off and cut my head open.

She explained that they would not cut open my head, but they would have to insert a plastic tube called a "shunt" to drain fluid from my brain and have it flow to another site for ease of elimination from my body. My mom did not want to hear this unsettling news. Frankly, neither did I.

The doctor told us that she and a radiation oncologist would determine the best drug for me. The drugs would be very potent ones (chemotherapy), which would run through my IV tube for a defined period in an attempt to destroy the bad cells. Then she would check my vitals after the first round of treatment to see if the mass in my brain was getting smaller. She explained that the chemotherapy treatments as a whole could last up to six months. The side effects might be unbearable sometimes. Sometimes the therapy might make me sicker than I was when I first came to the hospital.

I interrupted her to remind her that I was only ten years old and told her she was frightening my brother. I noticed he looked like he was turning green. But the real reason I reminded her of my age was that she had scared me out of my mind.

I looked at my parents and thought that my mom might pass out at any moment but noticed a smirk on my stepfather's face. I looked over at G-Mom. She was the only one who seemed to be holding it together. I expected G-Mom to question the doctor in many ways to get everyone to grasp how serious this was and how long it would take to see results. In a kind and compassionate way, my grandmother grilled the doctor like a drill sergeant! My doctor gradually realized that G-Mom was the stabilizing force in the family as well as very knowledgeable in medical terms. The doctor would frequently turn to my grandmother, seeking assurance that she was doing well explaining to the rest of the family and me. My doctor did not want to frighten my brother or me, but she felt we needed to understand the journey we were about to go on. I knew it would not be like the trip we had six months ago. I also knew that G-Mom would insist that I keep notes in my journal about my illness just as she did on our trips. I could not tell G-Mom that I had forgotten how to write.

This phase was really what my mom did not need to hear. The next step would be to target the terrain of the defective cells in any of the surrounding areas. A radiation punch would take about five minutes for each session and would be about five days in length; then they would test to see if it was making a difference. She told us that the side effects from a combination of chemotherapy and radiation therapy might be more weight loss, nausea, vomiting, and hair loss.

"Oh no, not my hair."

The doctor told us that some of my treatments could be done as an outpatient. I was happy to hear that I might be able to go home, but I saw the panicked look come over my mother's face. It made me sad to see my mom so afraid. Although she looked like she was concerned about me, I knew she was only thinking of herself. I did not want to put my mother through any more stress than she already had. This phase was what my mom could not bear to hear.

My doctor explained that there were experimental drugs that had been successful in a few cases like mine, but she would use those as a last resort if needed. When she said "last resort," I became terrified. I freaked out! Then the doctor explained that these would be clinical trials and that my participation would make it possible for other boys and girls to benefit from my testing the drugs if they worked on me. I think my mom did hear this but went into a rage again screaming, "You will not use my child as a guinea pig!" Mom embarrassed the whole family. The doctor did not know what to think and would not respond.

Of course, G-Mom stepped in and said she and the doctor needed to get out of the room to discuss my long-term prognosis. I did not know the meaning of *prognosis*, but I knew G-Mom well enough to know it was something big. Hearing that word made me nervous again but not a bad kind of nervous because I knew my grandmother had a need to know and would make sure everything was being done properly to take care of me. I also knew that she would explain prognosis through her clever storytelling when she felt the time was right for me to hear it. When the doctor used big words that I did not understand, I would glance at my grandmother.

The doctor's departing words that day were that we should prepare for long-term treatment. I looked at my stepfather and knew the discussion in our household would be tense that night. Knowing him, he probably would tell Mom that he had not signed on for this. Knowing Mom, she would start crying uncontrollably and try to appease her new husband. Knowing my brother, he would lock himself in his room and play video games so that he would not have to think about the bad news or hear Mom crying. Knowing my grandmother, she had already started making plans in her head to rearrange her life during this time to be near me.

By the end of this session with my doctor and family, I was wiped out. Through tears, I told my family I was tired and needed some sleep. My mom kissed me on the forehead and hugged me tight, which was rare for my mom. She was not a hugger, nor did she show us very much affection. My stepfather waved good-bye. My G-Mom smiled and said, "Sleep tight, kiddo, and don't let the bugs bite." I noticed she did not mention *bedbugs* this time. I made a note to ask her about that later.

As they began to leave the room, I asked if my brother could stay for a few minutes. I wanted to talk with him. I did not ask my grandmother to stay because I knew it would make my mom jealous and did not want to hurt her feeling any more than I had already by getting so sick.

When everyone left the room, my brother crawled into bed with me, and we hugged while uncontrollably crying. He told me not to worry, that he would take care of Mom. He also said not to worry because G-Mom would be in my room with me during the day as much as they would allow her to stay. We talked about our trip to Europe and what was going on in school and our new household. He noticed that I was tired so he told me he would come back to visit after school the next day. But he stayed until I almost went to sleep. When he did leave, I cried myself to sleep. I think this had to be the beginning of my journey and the worst day of my trip. I realized that I was very ill and had had no control over my drastic change in behavior for the past months.

Crack 8

THE POWER OF INSPIRATION

If there is no struggle, there is no progress.

—Fredrick Douglass

The greatest discovery of all time is that a person can change his future by merely changing his attitude...

—Oprah Winfrey

Chapter 10

A VISIT FROM CAPTAIN JEFF

The power of June's reflections can be unbearable.
It can be educational.
It can be sad.
It can be creepy.
It can be encouraging.
It can be the mirror in which to see an uncompromising will to live.
It can open up a world that one has never been to and will never go to.

The cancer center was June's world for eight months of her young life, a world that she kept closed from her family, only sharing it with her make-believe friends, Chemo, Rad, and Captain Jeff. Because her brain tumor was so rare, she was in a hospital more than a hundred miles from her parents' home. It was a specialty cancer center for children. So she had lots of time in her room with just her, her iPad when allowed, the TV, and more often than not, G-Mom.

June longed to see her pet, Lady Bird. Every time she asked about Lady Bird, the doctor would not allow Lady Bird to come for a visit.

Before her illness, she and Lady Bird were inseparable. When you saw one, you saw the other. Although Lady Bird was partially blind, she protected June in the neighborhood.

Lady Bird had no problem biting anyone she thought might be mistreating June. One time, Lady Bird bit a little boy who was bullying June. Another time, Lady Bird bit June's mother, Amy, when she pushed June out of a room, yelling and screaming at the top of her lungs.

Every night before going to bed, while on her knees, June said her prayers. Lady Bird would kneel next to her as if she was also praying. When June locked herself in her room every day to do her homework, Lady Bird guarded the door against Alex and warned her when her parents were in a bad mood and approaching her room. Her mother, Amy, treated the dog so badly that June decided to let her uncle keep Lady Bird while they went to Europe. When she returned from vacation, Lady Bird did not want to go home. June's uncle had spoiled her. June was thankful that Lady Bird would not be at home with her mom while she was in the hospital. June missed not having Lady Bird in her hospital room to protect her and to make her feel warm and fuzzy. She also missed having Lady Bird around to tell how she felt about her mother. While thinking about Lady Bird, June found herself falling asleep because she was exhausted.

JUNE HEARS VOICES IN THE DARK

A captain came to me in a dream that night—or at least I thought it was a dream. It was like when I said my prayers every night, I felt the presence of someone kneeling beside me. The person was invisible, but the presence was always there. When I finally woke up, I felt the presence of my grandmother, even though she was thousands of miles away from here. She had gone back home to take care of some business that could not wait. I told the nurses about a visitor who came to see me last night. The nurse said I was just dreaming, but her facial expressions showed her concern at what I was saying to her. I insisted that the visitor was real because he came every night around midnight. The nurse looked at me curiously and asked, "Why at midnight?"

I could not explain the time of my friend's arrival. There were no clocks in the room, but I always knew it was midnight.

Wherever I was or whatever I was doing, I was very sure that someone was in my room at midnight, sitting next to my bedside. The presence of my friend never made me nervous. In fact, I started to anticipate his arrival, as a calm came over me and I did not feel deserted and so alone. I decided to give my new visitor a name. At first, I wanted to call him "Zion." I have no idea where the name *Zion* came from except I am sure it was someone that I knew before Noma invaded my brain. Then I thought *Isaiah* would be a good name. I had no explanation of that name except it just appeared out of thin air. Isaiah had to have had some meaning in my life, but I just don't remember. But later, I liked *Jace* as the name of my visitor. Again, I could not recall who Jace was or why his name surfaced in my thoughts. Then I thought maybe I would call him Jeff. Even though I could not piece together how I knew a Jeff, I was sure that he was someone sweet, charming, funny, and overall a brilliant person. As hard as I tried, my brainpower could not allow me to know Jeff's connection to me. Since I came up with so many lovely names that I could not connect, I finally decided that I would call my new friend "Captain Jeff" because of how he made me feel. It was almost as if I was compelled to name my friend *Jeff*. The pull was unyielding.

Before morning came or sometime during my period of darkness, I encountered something that I don't ever want to see again.

I don't know where this image came from that was in my head. I was hiding out in a tree house that had lots of windows. It was far out in the forest, away from any homes. The tree house had been painted black. It had windows, but I could not see out of the windows. I remembered something G-Mom would say when someone died. "You have to open the window to allow the soul to float out to go where God needs it to go." My heart began to beat very fast. Sweat rolled down my head. My hands started to tremble. I remember thinking, "Please, window, do not open. Why are the windows dark? Is my soul ready?"

All of the grass around the tree house was dead. There were no flowers or trees remaining. Every time I opened the door, I could see a big ball of red light moving ever so slowly toward me, and I would immediately close the door. I could hear scratches on the window. I could hear whispering voices all around me.

Suddenly, I saw what appeared to be a peacock that was breathtakingly beautiful. The peacock landed on top of the tree house. Then, all the windows became abundantly clear. I opened the door and did not see the red ball anymore. I was standing in the middle of the tree house with just me and silence. I looked out the window and saw a beautiful patch of flowers glowing like a rainbow. Without warning, the darkness had turned to light and beauty. Was this another dream? Or was my brain playing bingo on me again? Was I supposed to escape the tree house?

The first night of Captain Jeff's visit, I had a long conversation about how I was feeling. Captain Jeff had a glow all around him. He never spoke a word. When he smiled, his teeth were as white as the snow on the mountains in Switzerland. I felt so comfortable in his presence. I closed my eyes and saw my mom sitting at the dinner table, laughing and enjoying being with her new family. I felt deserted. I believed that my mom wanted to punish me for getting sick because I changed their lives. I explained the hurt in my heart and told him that I was glad my mom had someone around her to make her laugh. Knowing that she was happy made me happy. The truth was I hated my mom, her husband, and all his children. But after I made a visit in the tree house, all of the bad feelings just went away. My shattered brain was playing tricks on me again.

My brother and I were so close, sharing everything with each other about how we felt. I so missed having him around me every day, but I knew he had to take care of Mom. Captain Jeff just nodded his head while I talked. Often, I told him that I did not understand why my mom did not love me. When she cried, they were not tears about me but about herself. My feelings toward my mom were not real emotions, and I knew that I had to overcome these thoughts to get well. Captain Jeff would not enter into the discussion. He was the best listener that I had ever met. He did not give me advice or tell me I was mistaken, which made me trust him more each visit.

On the second visit from Captain Jeff, I talked about sunshine and rainbows. The big truck with the sunshine face that we saw on the Autobahn appeared right before my eyes. I remember thinking when I first saw the truck as we were traveling down the Autobahn in Austria that it was the prettiest picture of the sunshine that I had ever seen. It was so cold that the sunshine truck was a welcome sight. I felt as if the sunlight gradually moved from the truck, engulfing me like a new baby wrapped in a blanket. The pain slowly disappeared. My mind told me that I was in my G-Mom's arms and she was singing to me, even though I knew that G-Mom had a terrible singing voice. I wondered, "Am I dreaming, or is this image real? How do I get my nurse to believe me?"

The third night of Captain Jeff's visit, I talked about family and memories of funny pranks we had played on each other. I told Captain Jeff about the time I put rats in my brother's bed. It scared him so much he wet his pants. I remember one time Alex put glue on my chair because he thought he was too old to babysit me. I sat in the chair for hours before we had to tell Mom what had happened. Mom beat Alex so bad it left welts on his back. I never told anyone about the beating.

On the fourth night's visit, I talked about good friends and happy times. I told Captain Jeff about my pet, Lady Bird. I shared with him how close my classmate Renee and I were. I told him about my classmates, but I could not remember their names except Renee. It frightened me that I could not remember who my friends were. I started to cry uncontrollably, but Captain Jeff never said a word.

On the fifth visit, Captain Jeff's presence reminded me of the vacation we had had in the Swiss Alps the early part of August before I became ill. Thinking about our vacation made me think of *Alice in Wonderland*, my favorite movie. Some of the houses in Switzerland were made mostly of wood, and they called them *chalets* rather than houses. I closed my eyes and could see the houses in the valley and treetops covered in snow. I saw mountaintops covered with snow as white as a lamb's coat. Tall trees peeked through with many colors. Castles and chapels stood on hilltops. Rock formations moved around like a picture of art. There was firewood neatly stacked on the side of houses. I saw cows grazing in the pastures, trembling from the cold while protecting each other against the raging wind. My vacation was the best that I remembered. When Captain Jeff finished his visit that day, I was smiling. He had transported me back six months when my life was so beautiful, filled with fun and excitement. I did not want this moment to pass. I could feel warmth in my body as I quietly slipped into a sea of blue clouds, twinkling stars, and a warm mist of rain. Peace. Be still!

Without warning, Captain Jeff did not visit for several weeks. I missed his daily appearance and nods. I think his presence gradually taught me how positive thinking helped me to heal. When I spoke about happy times, I always felt better. I spent that week talking to my friends Rad and Chemo. My doctor came for a visit and told me that it was important that Rad and Chemo be around this week. My doctor pretended that she believed I had imaginary friends. She suggested alternating the days they came to share with me. Chemo came on Tuesday, Thursday, and Saturday, and Rad would come on Monday and Wednesday. Sunday was a day she wanted me to sleep or a day of rest. I would lie in bed, looking at Chemo dripping and running through my veins, wondering what it would do to my brain. I had already started to forget important things. In order not to allow the family to know my memory was fading, I would pretend to be asleep when they were around. G-Mom recognized the changes so I could be "me"—whoever that was these days—around her. Alex suspected something was wrong when I could not call his name. He was so good not to say anything about my inability to remember his name, pretending that he did not notice.

Sometimes Chemo and I had long conversations about my drip while waiting for Chemo to do his magic. When Chemo went slow, we pretended that we were moving through a forest, admiring the beautiful rainbow of colors in the flowers lining the road. I think I saw these flowers when I was in Europe. When Chemo sped up, we would pretend that it was racing down the mountains we saw in Switzerland, except they were not as pretty. They were hard and ugly. I recall the only time my mom was happy was when she would walk around the house, singing and swaying to a song called "Purple

Rain." I looked up at the bags hanging over my head, and suddenly the liquids running into my body were purple. I thought it might be a message from my mother, and I hoped she was in the room with me.

I would share my innermost thoughts with Chemo when we were in the room alone. When a caregiver came in, we would stop conversing and I would pretend that I was sleeping. I did not want her to know that I shared secrets with Chemo. One day, I said, "Chemo, I am so afraid that I might not get better."

And Chemo said, "June, I am afraid sometimes too when I think that I am not doing a good job for you."

I would never let my parents or brother know I was scared. I always pretended to be brave when they were around, or I would pretend to be asleep. Sometimes when it was just Chemo and me in the room, I would cry or even scream, "Why me?" I could hear a voice telling me to be strong. I always heard a dog barking or whining. These things I remembered, but I could not get words out when the family was around. The silent voice in my head could only talk to me, and I could only share with Chemo and Rad.

My imaginary friends had become my only means of sharing what I was going through. I told Chemo about the voice, and he said it might be the voice of my grandmother, telling me to be who I am and be strong. One day, he jokingly said my brains were playing tricks on me. He even said it was my imagination. Chemo and I could talk freely like that. I counted on Chemo to always tell me the truth. One day, on a bright Thursday morning, I could not keep any food down. Chemo explained that he had to send more drips down, and they made me sick to the stomach. Even though my doctor had told me the same thing, I did not believe her until I heard Chemo's explanation. The next couple of days, the drip was faster. After the third day, it slowed down, and I felt much better.

JUNE THE PRUNE AND LADY BIRD

Rad knocked on the door.

I said, "Come in."

Rad was fat and grouchy. When I saw him, I could expect he would play around with my head. He always brought me a gift, usually something to put on my head. Rad told me that I would lose my pretty locks of hair, but I did not believe him. I would play games with him, pretending to have hair of various lengths. He would, in turn, bring me caps that always made me laugh. After about six visits from Rad, I woke up one morning, stretched, and scratched my head. I had a handful of hair in my hand. That explained why Rad had started bringing caps and wigs for me to try on. When Chemo came the next day, I couldn't wait to show him the hair, tell him what Rad said, and show him the funny caps Rad would bring me. I wanted Rad to be wrong. I needed to share my hair loss secret only with Chemo; after all, we shared everything.

Chemo said, "Your doctor needs to know about the hair."

I pouted and said, "No."

Chemo told me I was acting like a baby. After a long silence, I shared that I was afraid that I looked ugly and that my parents would be mad at me because they would think I cut my hair from throwing a temper tantrum. As usual, Chemo was reasonable. He convinced me that I looked "fresh" with no hair. We took pictures with my iPad of me wearing each hat Rad had given me. To soften the blow with my family, we sent about ten pictures to my mother with my caps covering my bald head. She e-mailed me back and told me how much they liked the pictures. The next day, I e-mailed my mom a picture of my bald head. Even though she knew I might lose my hair, she freaked out when she saw the picture. She Skyped me, and I could see the sadness in her face. I ended up cheering her up instead of her cheering me up. When the nurse came to wake me and give me meds, I had enough energy and clarity to tell her about the caps Rad brought me.

She smiled and said, "My dear June, you are dreaming again. There is no Rad, no dogs, and no caps around."

I faded back into sleep after taking the medicine she had for me. I don't know how long I slept. I could feel this strange thing inside my head taking over my thoughts. I had gotten too weak to fight it. It felt like playing a tug-of-war and I was losing. One day, this thing would be quiet, and then it would return with a vengeance. I did not know what to do. I was so scared that this thing would never let go. It sneaked into my path of vision and speech. I could still see Chemo and Rad but could not see or talk to my G-Mom. I felt her presence even while I was in the fight of my life and could hear her talking to me. That was the one thing I was sure off; I was hearing the voice of my grandmother. Even though darkness had control of my world, I could see and feel the calmness that came from Captain Jeff. I wondered, "What did I do wrong? Did I sin because I haven't been on my knees to say my prayers while captured in the tunnel of darkness?" I just didn't know. I wished Captain Jeff would send me a message to tell me it was OK.

Several times, I thought I listened to the bark of Lady Bird. But I knew they would not allow Lady Bird anywhere near me in my hospital room. Then I panicked! I thought maybe I did hear Lady Bird for real. Maybe Lady Bird and I had crossed over.

When I finally woke up, I could see images of a sweet old lady and a beagle. I thought I saw my room filled with senior citizens with white hair and sad faces. Did I send pictures of myself and my caps to my mom? Did I post a picture of me with my hair loss? Did she Skype me back? Why was the nurse saying there was no Chemo or Rad? Who are these old people, staring at me with tears rolling down their cheeks?

I could hear the voice of a person who was sobbing between words and immediately knew it was my mom. I knew I was awakening and moving back to reality when I heard my stepfather say, "You know, she would be better off if she did not wake up. We can't take care of a child that is as sick as she is."

Then I heard the voice of my mother say, "You are right, honey; I can't spend my time taking care of a sick child. She can stay with her grandmother. I can't miss work from bringing her back and forth for checkups. These treatments could go on for years. She has always wanted to be the center of attention. She can't come back to my house."

Even though my mom's words stung, I was so happy to be able to hear them because I knew I could give up Chemo and Rad; they had completed their tasks. They had outsmarted that thing that was inside my head. Thanks to my mother and stepfather's voices, I knew G-Mom and I would have a lot to discuss. I could tell her about my conversations with Chemo and Rad and about how scared I was when I was all alone for so many days in my world of darkness. Then, I slowly turned my head toward the voices, looked at both, and asked, "Where is G-Mom?"

My mother immediately realized that I had heard the discussion between her and her new husband. She desperately wanted to tell me that I was dreaming and did not hear what I thought I heard, but that would be an admission that they did say what they did. Mom started telling me how happy she was to see me awake. She said the color had begun to come back into my face. Mom began to cry uncontrollably. I knew it was fake. I knew she was crying tears of guilt, not tears of happiness. Unfazed by my illness, my stepfather appeared unconcerned. He said not a word, just looked at me with disgust on his face and made a stupid comment like he always did. I immediately heard my stepfather hollering, "Get that dumb dog away from me."

My Lady Bird had him by the ankle, biting and tearing the leg of his pants. Lady Bird jumped up and bit his hand. Attached to too many tubes and too exhausted to speak again, I just smiled at my Lady Bird, still defending and protecting me from harm. I was so proud of my dog attacking a *dog*. Suddenly, I realized that Lady Bird was actually in my hospital room. I was not in that dark place alone. She was wearing protective dog clothes, boot covers on her feet and goggles over her eyes, but her mouth was unsecured. If this was truly my Lady Bird, she was so cute. There was a mask on the floor. Lady Bird had taken it off to defend me. Alex had been sitting in the corner with his earplugs in, listening to music, but he jumped up grinning when he saw Lady Bird attacking mom's new husband.

Someone pushed the door open quickly. Lady Bird jumped into bed with me and gave me a lick on the face. Alex couldn't wait to tell him about what Lady Bird had just done. It was my uncle who had been taking care of Lady Bird for me. He was my grandmother's son, my mother's brother, and a licensed vet tech. He gave me a wink. That wink told me he had used his talent and influence to make it possible for Lady Bird to stay in the room when I was going through the treatments the doctors said would make me feel worse before I felt better. I felt comfortable because, like my grandmother, he understood the meaning of family and would do anything it took to help make me feel better.

As the day moved on, G-Mom finally came through the door. Oh, how I missed seeing her salt-and-pepper hair, her gracious face, her stylish shoes, her cool sunglasses matching the color of her outfit, and her briefcase hanging off her shoulder with her designer purse. My grandmother was a force to be reckoned with in a time of crisis. With the presence of my brother, my uncle, my dog, and my grandmother, I was now armed with my armor of protection. I looked at Grandmother. A tear dropped down the side of my face. I never said a word. G-Mom knew! She turned to my mom and quietly said, "You need to leave now. I will call you to keep you informed of June's progress."

My uncle chimed in and told Mom's husband not to let the door hit him in the back. Lady barked three times as if to say, "Yeah!"

Alex just stood there, admiring how G-Mom had handled the situation. I was thankful that Alex did not hear the bad things our mom had said about me not being wanted in her home. When my mom and stepfather left the room, all of my tourist friends rushed into the room and surrounded my bed. For the group, the tour guide had arranged travel to my bedside for those interested in giving G-Mom support while we went through this difficult time. From out of nowhere, forty old people with white hair, big grins, and hugs came into my room.

My doctor told us that the thing inside my head could have been deadly. As I listened to General Treehouse discuss my recovery and progress, I was unable to explain or tell her that no treatment could get rid of the conversation I had just heard between my mom and stepfather. Although the conversations with Rad and Chemo had dimmed, they flashed brightly in my memory and continued to weigh heavily on my heart. I guess my brain was still coming to understand the long-term effect of a mother who abandoned her flesh and blood for children not her own. To me, Rad and Chemo were real. I did not talk with them when anyone else was around. Captain Jeff paid me one last visit one night while I was asleep. G-mom heard me saying, "Thanks" and "Good-bye." She wondered whom I was talking to.

I told G-Mom about Rad, Chemo, and Captain Jeff, my unforgettable friends. She listened with close attention. I did not understand the look on her face. She asked me to tell my story to her several times over the next three days. She proceeded to tell me a story about her nephew Jeff, who had had a brain tumor similar to mine and was up in heaven. Was Captain Jeff my guardian angel comforting me during my time of darkness?

The day finally came to remove June from total parenteral nutrition (TPN) to being fed with first the tube inserted into her stomach and eventually food in her mouth. She had been in bed so long her new best friends became her physical therapist (PT), speech therapist (ST), and recreational therapist (RT). The RT would come into the sitting room with all kinds of crafts for the children to work on after they finished therapy. One morning, the kids decided to work on headpieces because all were bald girls and boys. They made three caps to look like their favorite cartoon. June, of course, made a hat for her dearest dog, Lady Bird, to match her cap.

The therapists had to teach June how to walk, how to hold her fork to feed herself, how to form words, how to wave her hands, how to hold a pencil, and how to turn on her iPad to play games. She referred to them as the "Triple T" team because she could not remember who did what. They called her the "comeback kid." After over 180 days of absence from her classroom, missing half of the school year, June was finally ready to come back.

Cracking the Final Code

THE POWER OF WILLPOWER

Where there is hope, there is a will.
Whether child or dog, where there is a will to do something, they will find a way to accomplish it.

*The future belongs to those who believe
in the beauty of their dreams...*

—Eleanor Roosevelt

EPILOGUE

G-Mom home-schooled June the rest of the school year. Her days were spent exploring various cities with her grandmother, Alex, Lady Bird, and her uncle; eating all kinds of food; buying new clothes; growing her hair back; and hanging out with friends. When school started, on the first day, her teacher read June's letter to the whole class again.

June found her peace and joy through an exit out of the dark tunnel she had called home for eight months. Life at her grandmother's house was finally giving her the chance to be a child who received unconditional love and affection.

Will June ever be able to forget her encounters while in her world of darkness?

June's return for checkups at the hospital extended to every three months instead of every month. June, Lady Bird, and Kayla were thankful for each day.

GRACIE BRADFORD

CONTACT THE AUTHOR

Thank you for your interest in purchasing this book. I hope you have been inspired enough to help kids with special needs become extraordinary.

If you enjoyed June, G-Mom, and Lady Bird's journey, please let others know about the book. Go to Goodreads.com or Reader's Favorite and write a review. If you purchased a printed book or downloaded an e-book, a review posting on the site where you bought the book would be helpful in developing future books in the Lady Bird series. Comments are welcome and may be sent directly to the author at gracie@authorgraciebradford.com or Twitter: @IamXordinary. You may also share your stories of beating the odds on my children's advocate page: www.Facebook.com/bradfordtrainforyou.

OTHER BOOKS BY GRACIE BRADFORD

Who Am I?—I Am….   *March 2014*

Through My Lens—I AM…   *March 2014*
A compilation of five fictional and non-fictional stories about children with diabetes, cancer, blindness, downs syndrome and severe physical disability coping with special needs in the classroom.

Lady Bird: Shawn's Sixth Sense   *January 2015*

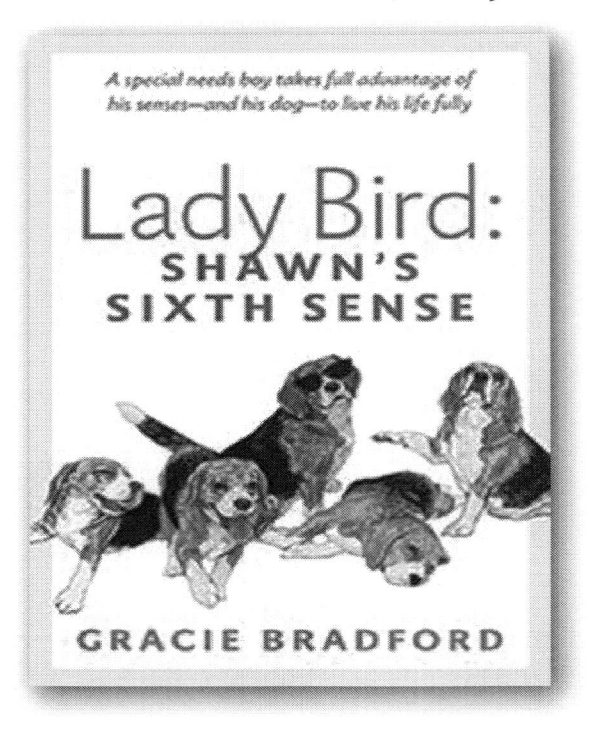

First in a series of books about Lady Bird, a beagle who is the hero in the story giving encouragement to blind children.

UPCOMING LADY BIRD RELEASE, BY GRACIE BRADFORD

Spring forward two years later, June meets ED, an experimental drug. Noma, the thing, is back! Lady Bird makes a new dog friend, who goes on the journey with her and June. June is taking experimental drugs to fight the spread of her raging disease. Lady Bird's new friend has human symptoms of autism. Lady Bird, June, and Alex are determined to improve their new friend's behavior. June finds comfort in watching the two dogs pamper her, each in his own unique way. Journey with Lady Bird, June, and their friends as they laugh, cry, hug, and ponder the why of the unknown. June also enrolls in a new school in Texas with her grandmother as her legal guardian and struggles to make new friends. Look for the third book of the Lady Bird series. It's coming in the middle of 2017.

ABOUT THE AUTHOR

Gracie (Specks) Bradford has witnessed her share of medical miracles. She started her professional career working in pediatrics medical nutrition and culminated her career as a senior leadership executive overseeing elderly patients and veterans in veterans' hospitals. When she worked in a large private acute-care hospital, she noticed that one of the patients had not talked to or interacted with anyone for months. One day, a visiting child came on the ward with his service dog. The dog wandered off and ran straight to this patient's room. Gracie just happened to be standing in the room when the dog came in and jumped on the bed. The expression on the patient's face was unbelievable. The patient wiggled his toes in unison with the dog's wagging tail. When the dog licked his face, smiles surfaced like sunshine. In that moment, Gracie knew she wanted to share the power of pet therapy—though it took her twenty years to find her passion for writing and tell her stories about the power of pet therapy in the healing process of children with special needs. Gracie asked herself, "Why now?" She answered with a "Why not now?" Thus came the birth of the character Lady Bird, an adorable beagle. Gracie never fails to mail Christmas cards and Christmas presents to her grand dogs instead of the dogs' owners.

Gracie is the mother of one pet-lover son and one daughter, and she is the grandmother to one mile-high grandson, one typical beagle grand dog, and one king terrier grand dog, who she swears has all the symptoms of attention deficit hyperactivity disorder (ADHD). She proudly honors her three sisters, who are schoolteachers and administrators, as women of noble professions.

Gracie graduated from Grambling State University, Grambling, Louisiana, and holds a master's degree from the University of Nebraska, Lincoln, Nebraska, as well as a master of business administration (MBA) from the University of Phoenix. Through her job presence, she has mentored and coached diverse employees, students, and patients at Scott and White Hospital in Temple, Texas; the University of Mary Hardin-Baylor in Belton, Texas; and VA hospitals in Chicago, Muskogee, Amarillo, Shreveport, Temple, Waco, and Alexandria. She is a member of Zeta Phi Beta sorority, the American College of Health Care executives, and the American Business Women Organization (ABWA).

Gracie is the CEO of her company, MBradford Management Associates, LLC, in Pearland, Texas. She retired in 2012 as medical center director with a goal to travel to all continents before 2017. Her hobbies include taking pictures of unique trees and flowers from around the world. And, of course, she never fails to find a single frog (not live ones) to add to her enormous frog collection back home in Texas.

Made in the USA
Charleston, SC
12 January 2017